To my granddaughter, Ella Ngala,
who stole my heart the first moment I saw her.

—A. Z.

WORLD'S Dumbest CROOKS 2

True Tales of Goofs, Giggles, & Gaffes

WORLD'S Dumbest CROOKS 2

True Tales of Goofs, Giggles, & Gaffes

by Allan Zullo

Scholastic Inc.

New York Toronto London Auckland Sydney
Mexico City New Delhi Hong Kong Buenos Aires

ISBN-13: 978-0-545-11664-0
ISBN-10: 0-545-11664-3

12 11 10 9 8 7 6 5 4 3 2 1   9 10 11 12 13 14/0

Printed in the U.S.A.

First Scholastic printing, September 2009

Contents

Criminal Hall
of Shame

Most crooks aren't smart, or they wouldn't be committing crimes in the first place. They're not exactly geniuses.

Unfortunately, even dumb bad guys often leave their victims shaken and upset. Thank goodness, criminal knuckleheads usually trip themselves up, making the police officers' job of catching them so much easier. Cops are constantly amazed at the folly and futility displayed by these fools.

In this book, you will read more than one hundred accounts of some of the dumbest crooks ever captured. All the stories are true and come from police files, court documents, and newspaper accounts. Among the dumbest of the dumb are:

■ **The fleeing gunman who got stuck in freshly poured cement.**

■ **The bandit who tried to rob a convenience-store clerk after giving her his driver's license.**

- The bumbling burglars who hopped into what they thought was their getaway car, but was an unmarked squad car with a deputy inside.

- The carjacker who led police on a high-speed chase until the road dead-ended into the parking lot of a state prison.

- The vandals who posted pictures of themselves committing their crimes on the Internet.

There is no shortage of absurdity in the world of criminals. And the best part is that their victims end up getting the last laugh.

Robbers

They Got His Number

A would-be robber of a muffler shop was so brainless that he gave the muffler shop employees his cell phone number and told them to call him when their boss arrived so he could rob him.

On a spring morning in 2008, the foolish crook, wearing a mask and waving a gun, entered the shop in Chicago and demanded money. The frightened workers told him the money was in a safe that only the manager knew how to open. And he wasn't there.

That's when the gunman came up with one of the stupidest ideas in criminal history. He gave the shop employees his cell phone number and demanded they call him when the manager arrived, so the manager could open the safe for him. They agreed and he left. It never dawned on him that they would call the police, which, of course, they did.

The cops stationed plainclothes officers in the shop, called the would-be robber on his cell phone, and told him to come down there. When he showed up again, he waved his gun around like before. This time, instead of scaring the workers, the plainclothes "workers" scared *him*. They whipped out their weapons and arrested him.

The knucklehead was charged with three counts of attempted armed robbery and one count of aggravated assault on a police officer. One veteran officer told reporters, "You can't make this stuff up."

Someone should have texted the crook, "U R an idiot!"

From Stick-up to Stuck-in

Memo to bad guys: If you're fleeing from the scene of the crime, do not . . . repeat . . . do not run through freshly poured concrete!

In Reno, Nevada, in 2007, a 30-year-old hotel guest was loading his luggage in the back of his truck when two robbers approached him. While one of them stood by the open driver's door, the other criminal pointed a gun at the guest and demanded his wallet and the keys to his vehicle.

The guest refused and began to scuffle with the gunman. During the fight, the gun fired into the air, causing the assailants to flee in a mad dash.

Hearing the gunshot, a police officer rushed to the scene and saw the robber with the gun running away. The cop gave chase and followed him into a building under construction. Without paying any attention, the gunman ran smack-dab onto a freshly poured concrete floor and became mired in the goo. While he struggled to get free, he was tackled by construction workers and arrested. The second suspect got away.

Out to Lunch

A teenager with no sense at all attempted to commit a robbery while his car was blocked in a fast-food drive-through line.

The would-be bandit drove his car into the drive-up line of a Taco Bell in Ashtabula, Ohio, in 2005. Even though there were cars in front of him and behind him, and there was a high curb on one side and the restaurant wall on the other, he figured it was the perfect time to rob someone and then drive off.

He got out of his car and walked up to the driver's side window of the vehicle ahead of him. Claiming he had a gun in his pocket—it was actually just his fingers—he demanded cash from the driver and the passenger, who were teenagers themselves.

When the victims gave him what few bucks they had, he became angry, so they offered him a skateboard. "I don't want a skateboard!" he yelled at them before stomping back to his car.

Seeing him get into his vehicle, the victims called 911 on their cell phone. The dummy was still blocked in the drive-through when the police arrived and arrested him. One of the cops recognized him as the Cleveland teenager who had been ticketed earlier in the week for driving without a license. If there had been a law against stupidity, he would have been charged with that, too.

Taxi Ride to Jail

Two teenage crooks in a convenience-store robbery might have successfully pulled off their heist if only they had their own getaway car.

A lone employee of the store in Oakville, Ontario, Canada, was talking on the phone to his wife when the two young men walked in late one night in 2008. They shoved the clerk out of the way and grabbed all the money from the cash registers. The thieves then fled from the store on foot. When they were a couple of blocks away, they called for a taxi.

What they didn't know was this: When they confronted the clerk, his wife heard the commotion over the phone before the call was cut short. She phoned the police, who went to the crime scene and learned that the robbers didn't seem to have a getaway car.

On a hunch, the cops asked a local taxi company to alert them of any suspicious calls from the area. Minutes later, an out-of-breath customer called for a taxi near the store, so the cab company alerted the police. Two cops met up with the taxi before the pickup, and one of them took over as the cabbie. When the taxi arrived at the pickup location, two young men emerged from a wooded area and said they had called for a cab. They were immediately arrested and driven straight to jail.

Detective Sergeant Kevin Maher, of the Halton Regional Police Service, told the news service Reuters, "Obviously, not having a getaway vehicle and calling a cab is generally not a sign of your most sophisticated criminal."

Dumb and Dumber

It's always dumb to attempt a robbery. But it's even dumber if you commit the crime across the street from the police station . . . and lock your keys in your getaway car.

On December 23, 2004, our dunce of the day wanted some cigarettes, so he went into a convenience store directly across the Lake Station, Indiana, Police Department and asked the clerk for three cartons of cigarettes. After she handed them to him, he bolted without paying.

When he reached his car, he discovered that he had locked his keys inside. The clerk followed him out of the store and confronted the crook, who then claimed it was all a joke, and that he didn't intend to steal the cigarettes. The clerk wasn't amused and returned to the store to call the police.

The crook ran back into the store and ripped out the telephone cord. Then he opened the store's lottery machine, took about 50 dollars, and fled again. Apparently, he forgot that his keys were still locked in his car, so he returned to the store again and grabbed a broom. He dashed outside and used the broom to smash the driver's side window. He opened the door, got in, and drove off just as a squad car arrived.

After a brief chase through snowy streets, the robber's car struck an oncoming police cruiser. He leaped out of his vehicle and promptly fell into a ditch where he was arrested on a felony count of robbery.

Wrong Place, Wrong Time

Two boys planning to rob a clerk chose the wrong place to attempt their crime—inside a police station.

One day in 2008, the boys, ages 12 and 14, walked into a regional station of the Port St. Lucie, Florida, Police Department. The 12-year-old sauntered over to the records counter where he picked up a phone to talk to a clerk who was sitting behind a protective-glass window. Then he demanded money.

"Not only did he pick up the phone and say, 'Put your hands up and give me your money,' he had his hand in his jacket insinuating that he had a gun," Officer Robert Vega told TCPalm.com news.

Instead of forking over money, the clerk alerted the cops who were in the next room. Within seconds, the kids were being handcuffed at gunpoint by a half dozen officers. The brainless crooks each were charged with attempted armed robbery.

"They were either very brazen or very dumb," said Officer Vega, "but I think it was the latter."

Photo Op

An armed robber ended up behind bars because he just had to take pictures of himself with a stolen camera phone.

In 2008, the thug and two of his fellow hoodlums robbed several patrons who were leaving a restaurant in Jacksonville, Florida. "He pulled a gun on us and told us he was trigger-happy and to give us everything we had," one victim told police. One of the things the robbers took was the victim's cell phone.

The next day, the victim bought a new cell phone that was able to access images that were sent to, or received from, his stolen phone. A few days after the crime, he noticed two new pictures had been downloaded to his new phone. After studying the images, he realized they were photos of the gunman. And the photos had been taken with the stolen phone.

He took his phone to the police and showed them the pictures the robber had taken of himself. In one of the cell phone pictures, the culprit was seen wearing a gold chain he had swiped in the robbery.

Police used the pictures to identify the assailant because he had a criminal record and a mug shot on file that matched the cell phone images. "He was brought over and interviewed by our robbery detectives," Jacksonville sheriff's office spokesman Ken Jefferson told reporters. "He initially denied everything until the pictures were shown to him, and he then implicated himself.

"It has to be one of the dumbest things a crook can do. He's charged with armed robbery. We don't have a dumb charge that we can put on him at this time."

Not His Day

This would-be robber should have just stayed in bed.

The 61-year-old man, armed with what looked like a gun, entered the Uihlein Soccer Park in Milwaukee, Wisconsin, one afternoon in 2006. He first tried to hold up a woman in an office at the sports complex, but she had no money. He left the office and then mugged a man who gave up his wallet—but there was no money in it.

Frustrated, the robber decided it was best to flee, but got lost in the huge sports complex and couldn't find the exit. People eventually realized the man's gun was fake, so they grabbed him and held him for the police.

Bad Advertising

For a robber, a getaway car should be as ordinary as possible so it won't attract attention. At least one armed robber didn't grasp that concept. He was nabbed during a crime spree because he tried to flee in his work van—one emblazoned with his name and phone number.

The lunkhead, who was a plumber from Monongahela, Pennsylvania, decided to rob a series of stores late one night in 2002.

First he drove his van to the Shop 'n' Go in West Elizabeth, Pennsylvania, and demanded that the clerk open her cash register. When she refused, he grabbed the register and left. About two hours later in nearby Clairton, he confronted a clerk at a Uni-Mart, saying he was armed and wanted the store's cash. When the clerk refused to follow his orders, he left without any money. Then he tried his luck several minutes later at another Uni-Mart. He was a bit luckier there. The robber grabbed some cash and drove off in his van.

There was, however, a problem. The store manager got a good look at the bandit's van—especially the plumber's name painted on the side and back of the vehicle, along with his phone number.

A Clairton police officer knew of the van and where it was usually parked. He waited in the dark until the vehicle pulled up at the spot, and he arrested the plumber as he got out of the van. The numbskull was charged with robbery, attempted robbery, and criminal mischief.

Allegheny County Assistant Police Superintendent James Morton later explained that the plumber's robbery spree went down the drain when the crook and the van matched the descriptions from witnesses at all three stores. Said Morton, "He made it pretty easy to solve by advertising himself."

Turn Right on the Road to Absurdity

A robber who led police on a high-speed chase after he held up a gas station did something stupid. He returned to the same station to ask for directions!

The nitwit, who was from Vancouver, Washington, brandished a knife as he walked into a Chevron station in Poulsbo, Washington, early one morning in 2004. After cleaning out the till, the robber and his passenger took off in a red Honda. But after an all-points bulletin was issued, the getaway car was spotted, and cops and sheriff's deputies from four towns gave chase. The caravan zoomed at speeds up to 100 m.p.h. through the winding roads of the western Puget Sound area, where twists and turns can leave even locals disoriented.

After a while, the fugitives managed to lose their pursuers in the darkness, but they had no idea where they were. So the stick-up man pulled into a Chevron station to ask for directions to Seattle, unaware that it was the very same establishment he had just robbed.

One of the attendants called the cops and gave the location of the suspects. They were soon caught and arrested.

Trading One Cell for Another

In his haste, an armed robber left his cell phone at the scene of the crime, so he foolishly went to the police station to retrieve it.

The 49-year-old Detroit man went into a Payless ShoeSource store in Farmington Hills, Michigan, one day in 2003. He walked up to the cashier holding a pair of black shoes and a small revolver, and then demanded money from the clerk. He stuffed $85 in his pocket and fled the store, dropping his cell phone on the way out. A witness turned it in to the police, who found the robber's address through a home number stored in the phone.

An officer called the crook and, without mentioning the robbery, told him someone had found his cell phone and that he could pick it up at the police station. The robber was dumb enough to agree to get it. Trying to trick the cops, he disguised himself by shaving his beard, donning eyeglasses, and covering his bald head with a hat. He arrived at the station to claim the cell phone. That's when he was arrested, charged with armed robbery, and tossed in jail.

"When you're dealing with criminals at this level, you find they aren't very sharp," Farmington Hills Police Chief William Dwyer told the *Oakland Press*. "He obviously made a lot of errors." Dwyer said it's hard to believe a suspect would walk into the police station just hours after he pointed a gun at a store clerk.

The robber had a 30-year criminal history and was a suspect in four recent holdups at area shops. "This guy is a career criminal," the police chief said. "He is also dumber than dumb."

Couldn't Lay a Finger on Him

Usually, an unarmed robber will attempt to trick victims into thinking he has a weapon. Not so for a masked man who tried to rob a pharmacy by openly shaping his fingers like a gun.

One night in 2003, the 30-year-old bandit walked into the Sniteman Pharmacy in Neillsville, Wisconsin, just as the store was closing. Whether out of laziness or stupidity, he didn't even try to stick his pointed finger in his pocket to fool the pharmacy owner, Bill Weiler, into thinking there was a gun. The buffoon simply held up his gloved hand and pointed his finger, with his thumb extended like the cocked hammer of a pistol.

At first, Weiler thought it was a joke when he was confronted by the thug, whose face was covered with a pulled-down stocking cap with eyeholes cut out. Weiler later told the *Milwaukee Journal*

Sentinel, "I kind of chuckled, 'This is a robbery?' and he pushed me and said, 'Yeah, this is a robbery.'"

Not impressed by the finger gun, Weiler, 55, wrestled the intruder down a flight of stairs. During the fracas, Weiler pulled off the guy's makeshift mask and recognized him as someone who had been accused of forging prescriptions at the pharmacy. The assailant escaped, but was arrested a few hours later. Prosecutors couldn't charge him with attempted armed robbery because a pointed finger isn't a weapon. Instead, he was charged with attempted robbery with threat of force.

Just Leave Your Name and Address, Please

What is it about criminals who witlessly leave their names behind at the scene of the crime?

A blockhead from Memphis, Tennessee, walked into a Perennial Realty's model home in Bartlett, Tennessee, on a Sunday afternoon in 2007 and pretended to show interest in the house. He even filled out an information sheet that listed each visitor's name and address. After looking around, he told the real estate agent that he was leaving but would return. Two hours later he was back, but this time he was holding a snub-nosed revolver. He pointed the gun at the agent and demanded that she hand over her gold-and-diamond-encrusted jewelry, valued at more than $23,000. When she did, he fled.

The gunman was easily caught—because he signed his real name on the information sheet. "Some criminals are not all that smart," Captain Tina Schaber told the *Commercial Appeal*. "We took that name on the sign-up sheet that he had filled out and then put that person's photo in a six-person lineup. The victim positively identified him as the person who robbed her."

The man was captured and charged with aggravated robbery.

■　■　■

Police didn't have to do much guesswork to identify a suspect in the armed robbery of a convenience store in Athens, Georgia, in 2008. They had his name, phone number, and address on the job application that he had filled out and left behind.

Authorities said that the 28-year-old lamebrain entered the Golden Pantry store and asked for a job application. He completed the form to kill time until he and the clerk were alone in the store. After the last customer left at about 11:20 P.M., the crook went behind the counter, pressed a steak knife into the clerk's side, and made off with the contents of her register.

When the police examined the crime scene, they found the job application. The witless robber had put down his real name and his uncle's real phone number. Police quickly tracked the thug down and arrested him. "It's kind of strange, but, yes, that's what he did," Detective Jeff Clark told the *Athens Banner-Herald*. Authorities said the dumbbell was also a suspect in several other armed robberies. He probably should apply for some other job besides armed robber.

■　■　■

A young man walked into the Git-N-Go store in Des Moines, Iowa, late one night in 2008. While he waited for all the other customers to leave, he took off his hat and jacket. Then, when the store was empty, he went up to the clerk and told him, "I have a gun. Give me all your money, and you won't get hurt." The shaken clerk handed over $115 from the cash register and watched the robber dash out of the store.

When the police arrived, they examined the hat and jacket that the crook had left behind in his haste. In one of the pockets, investigators found a tax form known as a W-2, which listed the person's Social Security number, address, full name, and where he worked.

Officers ran a check of the name on the form and found a listing for a 25-year-old with a suspended driver's license who was on probation for theft. The man's description matched perfectly with the one provided by the clerk. The robber was soon captured, giving him plenty of time to wonder if he would have to pay taxes on the money he stole.

■   ■   ■

A masked robber armed with a new AK-47 assault rifle charged into a gas station in Orlando, Florida, in 2007 and demanded the clerk hand over $75 and two cartons of cigarettes. The terrified employee did as he was told. Carrying his loot and his weapon, the gunman rushed out the door in what appeared to be a perfect getaway—except for one important thing.

When deputies arrived at the scene, they discovered that the bandit had left a gun case against a display rack. Inside the case, they found something important—the sales receipt for the new AK-47. Not only that, but the receipt had the name of the person who had recently purchased the weapon. So deputies paid a visit to the lamebrain, an 18-year-old who lived only a few blocks away from the station. When they raided his apartment, they found him, his mask, and the AK-47. He was arrested and charged with armed robbery.

Referring to an organization of people with exceptionally high IQs, sheriff's spokeswoman Susan Soto told the *Orlando Sentinel*, "Obviously [the robber] wasn't a member of the Mensa society."

■   ■   ■

Then, there's the case of the knife-wielding bandit who tried to rob a convenience store after giving his driver's license to the clerk.

In 2008, the crook walked into the Fegley Oil Co. convenience store in West Penn Township, Pennsylvania, and asked to buy a pack of cigarettes. The clerk refused to sell it to him until he could show proof of his age. So the guy handed her his driver's license. As she was checking his age—which was 23—he pulled out a knife and demanded money.

Sensing the goon was missing a few marbles, the clerk refused, saying, "I cannot give you money without a sale." Her response confused the crook, who eventually gave up trying to rob the store. He pushed the cigarettes back across the counter and left.

The clerk called the police and, when they arrived, she gave them all the information they needed—by handing them his driver's license. West Penn police obtained an arrest warrant, charging the man with robbery, possessing an instrument of crime, and simple assault.

Hey, Look Where You're Going!

For many criminals, the difference between success and failure is the escape route. It helps to keep your eyes peeled and to be aware of your surroundings. A clumsy purse snatcher didn't do that.

A woman was walking in downtown Des Moines, Iowa, early one morning in 2008 when a man pounced in front of her and threatened to slice her with the box cutter he held in his hand if she didn't hand over her purse. Fearing for her life, she gave him the purse.

As the robber began to run, the woman screamed with all her might. A passing motorist screeched to a halt and jumped out of the car to see what was wrong. Meanwhile, the bad guy, hearing the woman's screams, turned around to look at her while he was still running full speed.

Of course, if you're looking behind you, you're not looking in front of you. The mugger ran right into the side of a parked car so hard it nearly knocked him out. The purse and box cutter flew in opposite directions and landed on the sidewalk. The goon staggered to his feet and, swaying to his left and right, ran off—this time without looking over his shoulder.

The woman managed to retrieve her purse, which still held all of its contents. The parked car suffered big dents to the side and the trunk.

Going Nowhere

A purse snatcher who hopped into a getaway car didn't get away, because he forgot one important thing—gasoline.

In 2007, a woman was walking along the sidewalk in Hyannis,

Massachusetts, when a 19-year-old thug snatched her purse. The woman struggled with him before he broke free with the purse and leaped into a red pickup truck driven by a female accomplice. But they didn't get far.

A short while later, the same truck was spotted parked on the side of the road. When police went to investigate, the woman was sitting behind the wheel, and the stolen purse was lying on the front seat. When she was asked where her friend was, she replied that the truck had run out of gas, and that he was walking to the nearest service station to get some fuel.

While one officer stayed with her, a second cop found the purse snatcher walking back to the truck with a gas can. The officer offered him a ride, which he accepted, and then was taken into custody. After the purse owner identified him as the thief, he was charged with unarmed robbery.

A Fool for a Client

There's an old saying in the halls of justice: A person who acts as his own attorney has a fool for a client. How true.

During a trial for a 1985 armed robbery of a convenience store in Oklahoma City, Oklahoma, the defendant fired his lawyer. Court observers said the 47-year-old man on trial was doing a fair job of defending himself until Assistant District Attorney Larry Jones called the female store supervisor to the stand.

Jones asked her if she could identify the robber. She said, "Yes," and pointed to the defendant, who immediately jumped to his feet and accused the witness of lying. During his rant, he snarled, "I should have blown your head off!" After a moment of stunned silence when he realized what he had said, he blurted, "*If* I'd been the one who was there."

The jury took all of 20 minutes to convict him and recommended a sentence of 30 years in prison.

Idiocy in Evidence

A man from Wichita, Kansas, was arrested in 1996 for robbing a shoe store at knifepoint and stealing a $69 pair of size 10 $^1/_2$ tan hiking boots. Police were unable to recover the boots.

Three months later, at his trial, the birdbrain arrogantly rested his feet on the defense table. Judge James Fleetwood noticed the defendant was wearing a pair of size 10 $^1/_2$ tan hiking boots. The judge was incredulous. "I leaned over and stared," the judge recalled later. "Surely nobody would be so stupid as to wear the boots he stole to his trial."

It turned out that the defendant *was* that stupid. The knucklehead was convicted of aggravated robbery and sent back to jail—this time in his stocking feet.

Burglars and Intruders

Sore Point

A would-be burglar climbed over a fence to rob a house that he assumed was unoccupied. It wasn't. In fact, the owner was home, which was bad enough. Even worse for the intruder, the owner happened to be a sword-wielding member of Hungary's Olympic fencing team.

Virgine Ujlaky, 23, was practicing her swordplay in her house in a suburb of Budapest, Hungary, in 2007 when she saw the 43-year-old crook climb in through a window. She didn't scream or run away. Oh, no. Within seconds and a few swift slashes of the sword, Ujlaky pinned him against the wall. Holding the point of the blade against his throat, the swordswoman reached for the phone and called the police.

The villain was arrested 20 minutes later. Before the cops could take him away, he had to be treated by paramedics for shock. Said Ujlaky, "I wasn't scared when I saw him. It was good practice, because I have a competition coming up this week."

As he was led away, he reportedly complained, "Of all the houses I could have robbed, I had to pick the one with a fencing ace."

Car Fool

Two bumbling house burglars hopped into what they thought was their getaway car. What a shock it was for them to discover it was really an unmarked police cruiser—with a sheriff's deputy inside.

The bandits were members of a gang that had been plaguing the Naples, Florida, area in 2003. Burglars dressed from head to toe in black—hat, shirt, pants, socks, and shoes—were breaking into homes and stealing jewelry while the victims were eating dinner.

On this particular evening, the two intruders targeted a residence in a gated community at dinnertime. They pried open the rear sliding-glass door that led to the master bedroom and stole three pieces of jewelry valued at around $10,000. Back outside, one of them used his cell phone to call their accomplice, who was riding around the development in a gold sedan, waiting to pick them up.

Meanwhile, Collier County sheriff's deputies were patrolling the neighborhood searching for the burglars. One of the deputies was Sergeant Robert Maxfield, who was in an unmarked gold Taurus. While cruising the area, he spotted two men dressed in black emerge from a row of bushes.

Maxfield stopped the car. To his surprise, the two oblivious suspects ran right up to the vehicle, so Maxfield unlocked the doors. One of the burglars got into the front seat and the other one slid into the backseat. "Let's get out of here," one of them said.

Maxfield yelled, "Freeze! Sheriff's deputy!"

Realizing they had mistaken the police cruiser for their getaway car, the burglars bolted. Maxfield chased and caught one of the crooks, who was carrying a pair of gloves, a cell phone, and a small plastic mini-flashlight. He had an extensive criminal record as a burglar and was a suspect in other break-ins in Collier County.

The jewelry was recovered and returned to its owner. The 45-year-old burglar from Davie, Florida, was convicted and sentenced to ten years in prison. His accomplices eluded capture, no doubt rethinking their getaway strategy.

Lousy Cover-up

Two nitwits who burglarized their next-door neighbors' home might have gotten away with the crime if they hadn't displayed one of the victims' stolen possessions in their front window.

The simpletons broke into the home in Chalmette, Louisiana, in 2008 while the neighbors were away for several weeks. They took electronic devices and other items as well as a large blanket. Afraid that the victims, upon their return, might see the stolen items in the robbers' home, the thieves hung the blanket over their front window as a cover-up.

When the neighbors returned and saw that their home had been burglarized, they headed next door, planning to ask their neighbors if they had seen or heard anything suspicious.

That's when they noticed something suspicious—their distinctive blanket, which had a dog pattern, hanging in the window. So they called the police.

With a search warrant, the cops entered the suspects' home and found all of the neighbors' stolen items, which the telltale blanket was supposed to be hiding.

The burglars—a woman and her nephew—were arrested and charged with simple burglary and possession of more than five thousand dollars' worth of stolen property.

Said St. Bernard Parish Sheriff Jack Stephens, "This is like something out of 'The World's Stupidest Criminals.'"

Raising a Big Stink

When running away from the scene of the crime, a suspect learned, in a gross way, that a portable john at a construction site is not a good place to hide.

Police in Tampa, Florida, said that the 22-year-old crook broke into two pickup trucks at International Plaza Mall one afternoon in 2008. He stole a five-hundred-dollar digital camera and the owner's manual from the first truck. While inside the second truck, he spotted the owner and the owner's friend. The crook started to flee, and the two men ran after him.

Sprinting to a nearby construction site, he dashed inside a Port-O-Let where he thought he would be safe. But his angry pursuers saw him slip into the portable john. Rather than drag him out, they came up with a smellier idea: They turned over the Port-O-Let, so that human waste spilled on him. They held him inside the stinking mess until police arrived and arrested him on charges of burglary and possession of burglary tools.

Bungled Baubles

Burglars picked a good house to break into, making off with thousands of dollars' worth of jewelry. But of all the places they could have gone to sell their hot booty, they picked the only one that guaranteed their arrest.

The jugheads broke into the home of Ed Kanupp, of Newton, North Carolina, in 2008. Among the items they stole were a diamond tennis bracelet, a gold-leaf bracelet, and a ruby-and-diamond ring.

A week later Kanupp was at his shop, Goldsmith Jewelry Repair, in the nearby town of Hickory. A woman who was a regular customer came into the store carrying a plastic bag of scrap gold and a few pieces of jewelry that she wished to sell. Kanupp took the items out of the bag and began to arrange them by size. That's when he noticed some familiar pieces and realized he was looking at the jewelry stolen from his house.

It was difficult, but the jeweler tried to stay calm. He activated the silent alarm, which brought the Hickory police to the store, where they arrested the woman and a male companion who had been waiting for her outside.

The two, both from Hickory, were charged with breaking and entering and larceny. She was also charged with possession of stolen goods.

"I was hoping the jewelry would show up here," Kanupp told the *Hickory Daily Record*. "We discussed it at the house after the fact. My son joked, 'Dad, wouldn't it be the coolest thing if they brought the jewelry to the shop?'"

On the night of the burglary, the thieves failed to pay attention to the photos of Kanupp that were hanging on the walls of his home. The female crook certainly would have recognized him, having been a regular customer of his. If, by some chance, she did know whose house she was robbing, then she was a dunce to try to sell him back his own jewelry.

Taking a Bite Out of Crime

You've got to wonder what three dummies were thinking when they tried to burglarize a police-dog training facility.

Signs outside the building in Gainesville, Georgia, warned, CAUTION!!! GAINESVILLE POLICE DEPARTMENT K-9 TRAINING FACILITY — KEEP OUT.

Did the signs stop this trio? Nope. The two men and a woman were determined to dismantle the building's copper pipes and wiring. High copper prices in recent years have enticed thieves to break into buildings and abandoned factories to rip out the copper for resale. Despite the warning to stay away from the K-9 facility, the threesome broke in one night in 2007.

The building was an abandoned nursing home where the police-dog handlers and their canines held training sessions. "It's not like the place was a secret," Hall County Sheriff's Sergeant Kiley Sargent told the Associated Press. "I guess someone who is that determined to steal something might not pay attention [to the warning signs]."

As luck would have it, the threesome broke into the building on the same night as a K-9 training session. Seeing the cops and dogs enter the building, the culprits stopped ripping out the copper, dropped their tools, and ran. Foolish mistake.

"For anyone to try to run from a whole unit of canines, it's just a no-win situation," said Sargent. The 37-year-old woman proved to be the smartest of the bunch (which isn't saying much) when she surrendered before the dogs were ready to pounce. Her 18-year-old comrade tried to hide in a trash bin behind a nearby convenience store, but the dogs tracked him down and held him at bay until police collared him. The third criminal, a 39-year-old man who was obviously the dumbest of the bunch, tried to outrun the police dogs. He lost.

The three faced burglary and obstruction charges. The last one who was caught also faced a trip to the hospital for treatment of a dog bite on his rear end.

Deadbeat

A burglar who broke into a funeral home tried to fool police by playing dead. But two things gave him away: First, he breathed. Second, he wore grungy clothes rather than the Sunday best of those settling in for eternal rest.

Police in the town of Burjassot, Spain, said that in 2008 the 23-year-old suspect broke into the Crespo Funeral Home, looking to steal money even though there was none in the building. Neighbors living next to the funeral home alerted police when they heard someone force open the front door of the business in the middle of the night.

Officers arrived with the owner and searched the funeral home. Eventually, they found the suspect lying on a table in a glassed-in chamber used for viewings of deceased people during wakes.

"The custom here is for dead people to be dressed in suits, in nice clothes that look presentable," a police officer told reporters. "This guy was in everyday clothes that were wrinkled and dirty. He was trying to fake being dead, but he was breathing." The suspect, who had served jail time in the past for robbery, was caught "dead to rights."

Book Him

So, what does a dumb crook do when he's in a jam while committing a crime? Why, he calls the police and asks for help.

In 2000, the birdbrain called 911 about 2:00 A.M., begging for help because he couldn't get out of the Thomas Branigan Memorial Library in Las Cruces, New Mexico. When officers arrived, they spotted his shoe prints on broken glass, where he had gained entry by kicking in a windowpane. They found him trapped between the outer and inner doors of the foyer in the library. His hands were bleeding from dealing with the shards of glass from the window he had busted.

When police asked him what happened, all he would say was that while wandering inside the library, he became trapped between the two doors. He couldn't go back in and couldn't get back out. There was only one thing he could do: pick up the pay phone in the foyer and call police to get him out of his predicament.

"We couldn't determine what in the world he was doing in there because he invoked his right to an attorney and wouldn't talk to us," said Sergeant Joel Cano. "Sometimes, late-night studying just doesn't pay."

■　■　■

A 42-year-old chucklehead decided to break into the post office in North Fort Myers, Florida, one night in 2006. He lugged in a heavy sledgehammer and began whacking away at the drywall, trying to gain entry into the office area. After several sweaty minutes, he broke through the wall and squeezed his way inside. But once he got to the other side, he found himself trapped. No matter how hard he tried, he couldn't get back out.

The perplexed burglar was exhausted and out of ideas—except for one. He picked up the phone in the office and called 911. He told a dispatcher that he was locked in the post office.

When deputies showed up, he claimed that three men chased him into the post office. But his story was full of holes—just like the wall. He was standing next to the sledgehammer, he had a cut on one of his knuckles, he was seen on the surveillance video busting the wall and climbing through, and his footprints matched the ones in the dust in the office.

Detectives were quick to close the case and took the bumbling burglar to jail, where he was charged with burglary and criminal mischief.

The Tin(sel) Man

Police had an easy time catching a Grinch who cleaned out an apartment of its Christmas gifts. The cops simply followed a trail of tinsel that he left behind.

During the holidays in 2007, Boston police investigated a break-in. Someone had made off with 20 presents, a large flat-screen television, and several electronic toys. A witness in a neighboring apartment said she had seen a young man walk out of the victim's apartment with several wrapped presents. About 15 minutes later, the suspect returned and took out a large flat-screen television.

Police didn't have to go far to find their man. They followed a trail of tinsel from the victim's door that led directly to another door in the same apartment building. When officers knocked on the door, someone opened it. Then, as the police entered, two men dashed into a bedroom, slammed the door shut, and turned off the lights.

The cops explained that they weren't going to leave just because the men were hiding in the dark. So the suspects came out into the hallway, where one of them was immediately identified as the burglar. He was charged with breaking and entering, while the other was arrested on several outstanding warrants.

Bad Choice

Breaking into a building is never a good idea—especially if it's a police station. Yet, that's what two dolts tried to do.

One night in 2008 when the Gaston, South Carolina, Police Department substation was unoccupied, the intruders broke in by smashing in the back window. They intended to steal firearms, badges, and other police equipment so they could impersonate police officers.

But they were too noisy during the burglary, and a neighbor called the sheriff's department to report the substation break-in. While the intruders were rummaging around the office, deputies barged in and ordered them to put their hands up. The two men then fled out the front door, but were soon caught. One of them was carrying a Gaston police badge, gloves, and a police baton.

Both were charged with second-degree burglary. The two had planned the heist while they were in jail on previous burglary convictions.

Under Lock and Key

A crook who was attempting to burglarize a car ended up locking himself in the trunk of the vehicle.

One night in 2005, a security guard at an apartment complex in Fresno, California, followed a trail of blood from a vehicle to the back of another car. He heard banging noises coming from the trunk. Expecting to find a kidnap victim inside, he immediately called the Fresno County Sheriff's Department.

When deputies sprang open the trunk, the burglar climbed out and told them that he had been hit on the head and stuffed in the trunk. They didn't buy his story. Deputies discovered another break-in of a vehicle parked in a spot where the trail of blood started. The suspect was bleeding from a cut on his hand. And—surprise, surprise—what did they find inside the trunk where he had been locked in? Items that had been stolen from the other car.

Police said that, after burglarizing the first vehicle, the clumsy, bleeding thief broke into the second car by popping the lock on the trunk. Rather than reach in and take what he wanted, he tossed the loot from the first break-in into the trunk, climbed in, and ransacked every square inch of the trunk, a sheriff's department spokesman told the press. "But then he grabs the lid to the trunk to heave himself out and accidentally closes it on top of him. He's got to be the dumbest criminal of the day."

That guy is not the only half-baked burglar to lock himself inside a vehicle.

■   ■   ■

Late one night in 2002 in Gainesville, Florida, a lowlife unlocked a 1994 Infiniti and slipped inside. Seconds later, the car alarm went off. He tried to flee but couldn't. Of all the cars parked on the block, he had chosen the only one equipped with an antitheft device that automatically locked the doors when the car alarm was triggered.

Hearing the alarm, a neighbor grabbed his shotgun and ran outside in his boxer shorts. He saw the buffoon frantically trying to kick out the car's windows from within. The neighbor ran back inside and called 911.

When deputies arrived, they found the crook still locked inside the car. "He was trying to hide, all scrunched down in the backseat," Alachua County sheriff's spokesman Sergeant Keith Faulk told the *Gainesville Sun*. "I guess he thought deputies couldn't see him."

After arresting him, deputies found in his pockets a pendant valued at less than $50 and $3.21 in coins taken from the car. He was charged with one count of burglary and one count of theft.

Faulk told the newspaper that in 19 years of law enforcement, he had never seen a crook so dumb. "Maybe he needs a new line of work," said Faulk. "He's not very good at what he's doing now."

Faulk explained why this crook was so inept: "Had he pushed the [automatic door lock] button on the driver's side door, he could have gotten out."

Telltale Tattoo

A burglar ended up behind bars after making it way too easy for police to identify him. He broke into a car that was specially rigged with a hidden camera—one that clearly showed he was sporting a huge tattoo of his last name and date of birth.

The 21-year-old broke into a Peugeot 106 in a parking lot in Bristol, England, in 2008. Too bad for him that the auto was a "covert capture car," one of several that police rigged up to bait criminals. Inside each of these vehicles there were tempting items in plain sight that a thief would love to steal, such as satellite navigation systems, handbags, car stereos, and cell phones. In addition, each covert capture car was specially equipped with hidden cameras to catch the crook in the act. In two years, police arrested more than 200 people who tried to break into these honeypots, so named because the vehicles attracted thieves like honey does bears.

In this case, the cops' job of identifying the bandit was remarkably simple. He had vital ID information tattooed right on the side of his neck in big, bold letters and numbers—his name and birthdate. So when he made off with a stolen satellite navigation device, police knew exactly who the culprit was. He was no stranger to authorities, not with ten arrests over the previous few years.

Talking about the success of the honeypots, Police Superintendent Ian Wylie told reporters, "We get such excellent images from these cameras that there is often no doubt who the criminal is and what he is doing—and never more so than in this case."

Sleeping on the Job

A burglar had such a busy night breaking and entering into homes that he got tired. So, after taking other people's things, he decided to take one more thing—a nap inside the house of one of his victims. Boy, did that sleepyhead wake up to a big surprise.

One night in Missoula, Montana, in 2007, a homeowner flagged down police and told them there was a strange man sleeping in his basement. Cops entered the house and quietly made their way downstairs, where they found the intruder lying on the floor, snoring away. In fact, he was so deep in dreamland that the cops couldn't wake him up. Not until they yelled at him and threatened to Taser him did he finally open his eyes and realize that he was caught in a real-life nightmare.

Next to him was his black bag loaded with all kinds of evidence—obviously stolen stereo equipment and a wallet. Rather than admit that he had been caught red-handed, he tried to lie his way out of trouble by claiming he had gotten drunk at the homeowner's party and was just sleeping it off. That story didn't wash because the homeowner was standing right next to the cops and said there had been no party.

The bad guy was hauled away and charged with felony theft and burglary. He faced the strong possibility that he would catch up on his sleep behind bars.

■　■　■

Police in Oak Lawn, Illinois, were called to an apartment complex's parking lot in 2006 to investigate a series of burglaries of cars that had been broken into during the night. While they were interviewing the victims, a man came over and told them that someone had broken into his pickup and was still inside it, sound asleep and curled up around a pile of loot on the passenger seat.

The cops woke up the intruder, pulled him from the truck, and searched him. They discovered that the 30-year-old was carrying several items that had one thing in common—they were all reported missing from the burglarized cars parked in the lot. Stuffed in his pockets were the wallets of two men whose cars had been broken into. A screwdriver, a flashlight, a pair of scissors, and a plastic baggy filled with $23 in loose change also were found on him.

The crook, who was on parole from a previous burglary conviction, was tossed in jail, where he faced two new felony burglary charges. Too bad for him he didn't drink a few cups of coffee before he went on his crime spree.

Calling One's Bluff

A pair of would-be burglars tried to throw off police by reporting the crime to the cops. No need to guess how that worked out for them.

According to the Vermilion, Ohio, Police Department, in 2008 a call came in from a teenage boy reporting that the house next door had been broken into by two masked males. "The boy who called claimed to be a witness who saw people entering the house," Vermilion Police Lieutenant Richard Labis told the *Elyria Chronicle-Telegram.* "He gave the dispatcher a detailed description . . . and what they were wearing."

When the cops arrived at the scene, no one was home. However, they talked to the teenager who lived next door and had called in the crime. He was with his buddy. "There were two juveniles outside during this time, and officers noticed their clothing matched the description of the clothing given to our department," Labis said.

Police began to suspect something fishy. "We found muddy prints inside the house and footprints in the snow-covered backyard that matched shoe prints of one of the two boys," Labis said. "Nothing appeared to have been taken, and the homeowner said it did not appear that anything was disturbed."

After talking with the two so-called bystanders, the teens admitted they broke into the home. They didn't exactly explain how they thought calling the police would help them. "They apparently figured they could throw us off the trail," said Labis.

Instead, the two boys were thrown into the Erie County Detention Center and charged with burglary.

In a Tight Spot

A dimwit who was trying to burglarize a pharmacy by entering through a rooftop air vent wound up crying for help after becoming stuck in the shaft for 12 hours.

One night in 2007, the 25-year-old burglar went to the back of the CVS Pharmacy in Silver Springs Shores, Florida. He stacked pallets and climbed up a square gutter pipe to the roof. The thief, who was five feet five inches tall and weighed about 130 pounds, then pried off a ventilator fan and used a rope to climb into the opening.

Everything was going exactly as he planned . . . until the rope unraveled, and he fell 15 feet before getting wedged in the narrow metal shaft. His hands were over his head, and his feet were stuck on some pipes. And that's where he stayed throughout the long night. As he tried to wriggle himself free, his sweatpants slipped off.

About 7:45 A.M., a delivery man, who had been stocking milk before the store opened, walked into the men's room and heard strange banging noises above the ceiling and someone yelling, "Help! Help!" The delivery man went upstairs into a storage area to investigate and heard a frantic voice say he was stuck inside the air vent. The delivery man alerted the store manager, who went into the women's restroom and saw a busted ceiling and a pair of sweatpants hanging down. The manager called 911.

The burglar "was begging the manager to help him out," recalled Marion County Sheriff's Captain James Pogue.

After assessing the situation, the sheriff's office called in Fire Rescue's Technical Rescue Team, which needed an hour and a half to free the trapped dummy. Rescuers worked the problem from three angles. One group monitored him from the roof; a firefighter, standing on a stepladder with his torso through the restroom ceiling, secured him from below; and a third group broke through an upstairs wall and cut open the ductwork.

According to the *Ocala Star-Banner*, at one point during the rescue, the fool pleaded with rescuers, "Please get me out. I'm ready to go to jail. Just get me out."

When they finally cut him free, rescuers eased the burglar to the ground. The man, who was in boxer shorts and had badly scratched bare legs, was placed on a gurney behind the CVS store. While he was still on the gurney, he told reporters that he had gone into the ventilation shaft because he was trying to rescue a cat. "I heard a cat in the thing," he said. "I was trying to chase the cat."

No one believed him. The chump was charged with commercial burglary, possession of burglary tools, and felony criminal mischief.

For Goodness' Snakes!

Of all the things a burglar might want to steal, you'd think deadly live snakes wouldn't be on his list. Well, it was right at the top for one blockhead.

According to the Sumter County, Florida, Sheriff's Department, a 20-year-old burglar went to the back of the home of a snake breeder in

Bushnell, Florida, in the middle of the night in 2007. He ripped open the aluminum door of a shed, ignoring the sign in red block letters that warned there were poisonous snakes inside. He grabbed five snakes—including two poisonous rock rattlesnakes.

At some point, the burglar paid dearly for his theft when one of the rattlers bit him on the hand, causing a gash, not to mention lots of pain. For some unexplained reason, the featherbrain chose not to go to the hospital. Instead, he went to the local Wal-Mart later that morning.

When store employees saw a man wandering around their store with bloodstained clothes, they became suspicious and called the police, who first thought he had been wounded in a fight or from a gunshot. But then they discovered he had been bitten by a snake. The cops searched his car and found boxes containing the five stolen snakes.

The culprit was airlifted to Orlando Regional Medical Center for medical treatment. The snakes were returned to the owner, who told reporters that the burglar had picked the wrong reptiles to steal. "I've got an albino boa that's six feet long," the owner said. "If the guy knew what he was doing, that would have been a good snake to grab."

True, but if the burglar had stolen the constrictor, he might have ended up in a tight squeeze.

Rude Awakening

It's important to eat a good meal and get plenty of sleep before going to work.

A 52-year-old dunce who hadn't eaten or slept in quite a while burst through the kitchen window of Cathy Ord, 60, and Rose Bucher, 63, while they were relaxing in their house in Tampa, Florida, one night in 2003. He waved his sawed-off shotgun and announced he was there to rob them.

But rather than grab valuables and leave, he lingered because the women didn't act frightened of him. He was moved by how friendly they were, considering he was an armed man who had just broken into their home.

"We just treated him with kindness," Bucher told reporters later. "He said he wouldn't harm us unless we did something stupid." The robber ordered the women to turn off the lights and to talk in a whisper. He sat on their couch for a long time chatting with them, all the while holding his weapon.

When he admitted he was hungry, they made him a ham sandwich and gave him a bottle of rum to wash it down. "It was so surreal," recalled Ord. She offered him cash and the keys to her Cadillac, but he didn't want to leave. So they encouraged him to keep eating and drinking.

Finally, about 3 A.M., he asked them to call him a cab. By the time it arrived, he was asleep on the couch, so they called 911. When the gunman woke up, he was surrounded by more than a dozen sheriff's deputies.

They tossed him in jail without bail and charged him with armed home invasion and false imprisonment. At least behind bars, he was able to get three squares a day and plenty of sleep.

Homebody

A burglar picked out what he thought would be the perfect house to break into. But he didn't enter through a door or window. He decided to go down the chimney like Santa Claus. Ho, ho, ho turned into *oh, oh, oh.*

The five-foot-seven-inch, 150-pound bonehead climbed up the roof of a house in Dallas, Texas, late one night in 2008 and figured he was small enough to fit down the chimney. He wiggled his way into the opening and promptly got stuck. He couldn't move up or down, so he began yelling, "Help me! Help me!"

The next-door neighbor first heard his cries for help about 5 A.M. But she didn't realize what she was hearing for several hours. When she finally discovered that the shouts were coming from the house, she called out, "Where are you?"

"I'm up here!" he replied.

She phoned 911. Firefighters quickly arrived and worked for hours to free him. Brick by brick, they dismantled the chimney until they were able to lift him out with a rope. He was taken to Baylor Medical Center for treatment and then right to jail.

And here's the clincher: The house was for sale, and the owners had already moved out. There was nothing inside to steal!

It Went Thataway

A burglar discovered that it's pretty hard to flee the scene of the crime when his getaway car went thataway.

The 26-year-old crook tried to break into a house in Little Ferry, New Jersey, in 2008. But he was thwarted by the homeowner, so he took off running. He decided against hopping into his car and getting out of the neighborhood. Instead, the dolt went prowling for a different house to rob.

Meanwhile, the homeowner of the first house called the police, who began scouring the area for the intruder. The cops found his car parked near the house. Inside the vehicle was a backpack that contained gold coins, jewelry, and cash—items from previous burglaries. Police had it towed away.

After the burglar's attempt to break into another house failed, he headed back to the spot where he had parked his car—and where police were waiting. He was shocked to see that his car was missing. He was even more shocked to see that the police had surrounded him.

"He had no way to get away," Police Chief Ralph Verdi told *The Record* of Bergen County. "His car was gone an hour before that."

The fool confessed to burglary, attempted burglary, and possession of stolen property.

Said the police chief, "Thank God for dopey burglars."

Big and Little

A couple of lamebrained thieves got caught because they didn't have a car big enough to carry their booty.

Police in Middletown, Ohio, were investigating a burglary at a TV and appliance store in 2006. The window in the front door had been smashed in, and a 55-inch Hitachi flat-panel TV had been taken.

A half hour later, the cops saw a Mercury Sable driving down the street with one of its back doors open. They stopped the car and discovered a 55-inch Hitachi flat-panel TV hanging partially out the open door.

The police arrested a married couple. The husband was charged with breaking and entering and felony theft. His wife was charged with being an accomplice. They would have gotten away with the crime if only they had chosen a smaller TV or driven a larger car.

What a Cutup

One burglar was just not cut out for a life of crime.

In 2004, an 18-year-old knucklehead smashed a glass door at a closed gas station on Whidbey Island, Washington. As he gained entry, he cut his hand badly and began bleeding all over himself and the store.

When he couldn't open the cash register, he stuffed his pockets with packs of cigarettes and left. He returned to the store three minutes later and again tried, but failed once more to open the cash register. So he shoved more cigarettes into his pockets.

By this time, he was getting weak from loss of blood. He needed help, so he did the only thing he could think of: He called 911. Officers found him lying on the floor, with blood on his jacket and throughout the store.

He told them he had tried to break up a burglary, but was beaten with a bat by two men who drove off in a sports car. The officers didn't buy his tale, especially when they found the stolen cigarettes in his pockets. Their suspicions were confirmed when they viewed the store's surveillance camera, which caught the one-man break-in on tape.

The nitwit was booked on two counts of second-degree burglary—

one count for each time he entered the store.

"Criminals are not particularly smart," Island County sheriff's spokeswoman Jan Smith said in an understatement. "That's how they get caught."

Fare Not So Well

A simpleton tried to use a cab as his getaway car.

In 2002 in Holland, Michigan, a 20-year-old burglar broke into a residence while the victim was out and took a computer, a TV, a stereo, a Sony PlayStation, and two camcorders. Realizing he couldn't carry everything away with him, he used the victim's telephone to call Red's Taxi. When the cab arrived, he loaded up the loot.

In answer to the driver's question about the items, the bandit replied that he was moving. The cabby became suspicious after his fare asked to be dropped off in an alley.

When the victim reported the burglary, a witness remembered seeing a taxi parked nearby about the time of the crime. Investigators went to Red's Taxi, checked the dispatch logs, and arrested the crook at his home a few hours after the burglary. Police recovered all the stolen property there. The perpetrator was charged with second-degree home invasion.

Car Thieves and Carjackers

Dead-end Job

A dense carjacker discovered he should have used a road map.

Threatening a female driver at knifepoint, one day in 2003, he forced himself into her car at a gas station in Lancaster, California, and ordered her to drive off, which she did. After she drove a short distance, he kicked her out. Once he got behind the steering wheel, he began weaving in traffic, which caught the attention of a Kern County deputy sheriff, who tried to pull him over without success.

The carjacker floored the accelerator, setting off a high-speed chase that eventually involved several more police cruisers. When he turned onto Highway 202, he hit speeds of more than 100 m.p.h. He thought he could outrun the cops. Maybe he could have if he had chosen a different road.

Guess which state highway dead-ends at a state prison? Yep, it's Highway 202. The carjacker drove his car right into the front parking lot of the California Correctional Institution in Tehachapi. With a dozen cop cruisers behind him and a dozen prison guards in front of him, he had nowhere to go.

But he wasn't through being brilliant. He took himself hostage. Holding a knife to his neck, he told the police that they better let him go, or he would cut his throat. When the laughter died down, a sympathetic cop convinced him to drop his knife and put on some handcuffs.

He was charged with kidnapping, assault, and carjacking. When the court was through with him, he went to serve time at the dead end of Highway 202.

Such a Deal

A thief who stole an SUV from a used-car lot must have left his brains behind, because he returned to the same business a month later, trying to trade in the same hot vehicle for a nicer car.

In March 2007, the crook came to Wholesalers of America in Norwalk, Connecticut, wanting to test-drive some vehicles. But there was a problem with the man's credit, so salesmen at the dealership wouldn't let him take any test drives.

Sales manager Diego Coleman told the *Stamford Advocate* he last saw the suspect wandering around the lot by a 2003 Jeep Liberty that was being prepared for a customer who had just bought it. The keys were in the unattended vehicle. A minute later, the Jeep and the suspect disappeared.

Coleman assumed he would never see the vehicle again. So imagine his surprise when the numbskull showed up at the dealership a month later with the stolen Jeep and wanted to trade it in for a larger vehicle.

"I was left speechless," Coleman told the newspaper. "I couldn't believe that he would try to bring back the car and not think we would recognize him."

Salesmen stalled the thief while Coleman called the police. When the cops inspected the vehicle, they were amazed that the crook made no effort to hide the fact that the Jeep had been stolen from the dealership. They found that the key ring was the same as those issued to new customers by Wholesalers of America. The temporary license plate on the vehicle had been issued to the dealership, and documents found in the glove compartment showed the SUV belonged to the dealership. Even the vehicle identification number had not been tampered with. The crook was charged with car theft.

Said Coleman, "There's got to be something wrong with this guy to come back and try to sell us our own vehicle less than two months after he stole it."

Driven to Desperation

A couple of dim-witted but persistent car thieves drove themselves nuts.

One night in 2005, the thieves used a crowbar to break into the showroom of Manteca Ford in Manteca, California. They rifled through the dealer's offices until they found the safe with the car keys, which they managed to crack open.

They found the key to the one car they wanted more than any other—a red Ford GT. Thrilled they had the key, they hopped into the car, which was on the showroom floor, and tried to start it. Just their luck, the battery was dead. Ah, but they weren't deterred. They found a battery charger and juiced up the car's battery.

Before they could drive the car out of the showroom, they had to push a Mustang GT (which, by the way, belonged to rapper 50 Cent) out of the way. They opened the showroom's double doors and revved up the car. In their zeal to leave, the bandits unwittingly learned why drag strips aren't made of tile. When the driver gunned the accelerator, the tires squealed and the car fishtailed on the slippery floor, slamming into the frames of the showroom doors and damaging the sides of the Ford GT.

Now that they were finally out of the showroom, the thieves

zoomed all the way . . . to the end of the parking lot. The gates were locked. The persistent crooks refused to give up. They returned to the office and grabbed another set of keys, this time to a Lincoln Navigator and used the luxury SUV to ram open the gates.

Okay, now they were ready to take this baby on the road. Laying rubber, the red Ford GT roared out of the lot and promptly ended up in a one-car wreck that caused $30,000 in damage. After all that effort and overcoming all those obstacles, the lunkheads didn't know how to handle the 550-horse muscle car.

Get the Picture?

Crooks—at least the dumbest ones—just can't resist the opportunity to take pictures or videos of themselves breaking the law.

In 2006, a yellow 1995 Ferrari 355 Challenge car, valued at about $125,000, was reported stolen in Plaistow, New Hampshire. Police had few leads. But during a separate investigation, they arrested a 27-year-old man on charges of stealing and dismantling vehicles, then reselling the parts.

Police questioned him about the missing Ferrari, but he denied any knowledge of its whereabouts, claiming he had nothing to do with its theft. Ah, but his cell phone proved otherwise. When police examined his cell phone, they were intrigued with its screen saver. It pictured the suspect behind the wheel of the stolen yellow Ferrari.

"It's very difficult when a client proclaims his innocence, but incriminates himself by taking photos of the stolen items," his defense attorney, William Korman, told the *Wall Street Journal*.

The car was recovered intact in a storage unit in Merrimack, Massachusetts, leased by the crook. He pleaded guilty and was sentenced to five years in prison.

Next Time, Take a Hike

Talk about a loser. A two-bit criminal was released from jail, so what does he do just seconds later? He tries to carjack a sports car in the jail's parking lot.

He managed to toss out the driver and hop in, but he didn't go anywhere. The birdbrain didn't know how to drive the vehicle because it was a stick shift.

In 2008, the 21-year-old goon from West Palm Beach, Florida, was arrested by Riviera Beach police on a misdemeanor trespassing charge. Taken to jail, he went before a judge, who released him a few hours later on his own recognizance (meaning he didn't have to put up any bail money).

But just moments after he walked out of the Palm Beach County jail, he saw a gleaming silver Nissan 350ZX . . . and he wanted it. Never mind that it was broad daylight with people around, and he was in the jail parking lot. He wanted that sweet sports car. The driver, a 23-year-old woman, had just parked her vehicle, because she planned on visiting someone in jail. She was getting out of the 350ZX when the culprit ran over to her, yelling at her to give him the car. She refused and began screaming for help.

"There was a struggle," sheriff's spokesman Paul Miller told reporters later. "The guy was able to get the keys away from her and put them in the ignition. But it was a five-speed shift, and he didn't know how to drive it. That's why he couldn't get away from the parking lot."

The carjacker was still grinding the gears when a pistol-packing priest from the sheriff's office, who regularly visited the jail to mentor prisoners, rushed over. Whipping out his gun, the priest made the thug get out of the car and lie facedown on the ground until a deputy arrived and handcuffed him.

Instead of being free and having to deal with only a no-bail misdemeanor from his earlier arrest, the fool now was locked up under a $50,000 bail and facing a much more serious charge of felony carjacking.

When deputies asked him why he would attempt such an idiotic crime only moments after his earlier release from jail, the crook said he just didn't feel like walking the six miles back home.

Map Flap

It's no wonder this car thief got nabbed. He was with the stolen vehicle when he stopped and asked a uniformed police officer for directions.

The lamebrain, who was from Asbury Park, New Jersey, had driven the stolen car to Alabama and was on his way to Virginia when he got lost in Indiana in 2006. He pulled into a rest stop on Interstate 65 near Edinburgh, Indiana. Rather than ask a fellow motorist for help, he sought out a state employee—Indiana State Police Trooper Tommy Walker. It certainly wasn't the wisest choice, considering the thief was driving a stolen car, and Walker was in uniform and in a marked squad car.

"He waved me down carrying an Indiana map," Walker told a reporter later. "He said he wanted to get to Richmond, Virginia."

Walker gave the man directions to Virginia, but there was something about the man's behavior that triggered the cop's curiosity. As the man headed back to his car, Walker checked the vehicle's license plate and found it had been stolen from Bradley Beach, New Jersey.

The trooper then arrested him on a charge of possession of a stolen vehicle. The thief claimed the vehicle belonged to a friend. Walker recalled, "He asked me why he would come to me if he was driving a stolen vehicle." Maybe it was because he was a few pints shy of a quart.

A New Meaning for "Cell Phone"

After a bad guy robbed a man of his money and car keys, the thug stuffed him into the trunk of the victim's car. Then the culprit drove the vehicle to a bank ATM to take money out of the man's checking account. The crime was going exactly as planned. That is, until he was suddenly surrounded by cops.

Like many crooks, he made a serious blunder. He forgot to thoroughly search the man he was robbing. If he had, the assailant would have discovered the victim's cell phone and taken it away. But he didn't, so the victim was able to call police.

According to the Ohio *Columbus Dispatch*, attorney Ira Sully, 59, was working late one night in 2007. While he was walking from his office to his 2003 Chevrolet Cavalier, Sully was confronted by a gunman whose face was covered by a bandanna.

"Give me everything you've got," the robber demanded. "Do as I say because you don't want to die."

The goon took Sully's wallet and keys and then forced him to lie on the ground where, under the threat of death, the attorney gave him the PIN of his bank card so the assailant could withdraw money from the victim's account. Next, the thug opened the trunk of the Chevy and ordered Sully to get inside it. After Sully did as he was told, the trunk lid slammed shut.

The robber drove the car toward the bank, gloating over what had so far been a perfect crime. It never dawned on him that his victim had a cell phone. At the bank ATM, the gunman withdrew money from his victim's account. He got back in the car and started to drive.

Even though Sully knew how to release the trunk lid from the inside, he decided against opening it and making a run for it. Instead he called 911 and told the dispatcher, "I've been kidnapped and robbed, and I'm in the trunk of my car." Sully described the robber and his car to the police.

Less than two minutes later, cops spotted the car and pulled it over. After ordering the driver out at gunpoint, they opened the trunk and freed Sully, who was not harmed. All his money that had been withdrawn from the ATM was recovered.

The culprit was charged with aggravated robbery and kidnapping. He was convicted and soon behind bars in a case that gave new meaning to the term *cell phone*.

Low on Intelligence

Two dumbbells who stole a car from a worker at a service station soon realized that the vehicle was low on gas. So what did they do? They returned to the station to fill it up!

Pam Pease, who worked at the Parade gas station in Pensacola, Florida, was dismayed one day in 2005 because two men who had been lingering at the station hopped in her car and took off. She promptly called the police.

An hour later, she was sweeping the parking area when she noticed a familiar car pull up to pump number 7. It was her blue 1994 Ford Escort with a missing hubcap. "It just blew my mind, but there they were," Pease told reporters later.

Another attendant, Vince Nguyen, recognized the suspects as the ones he had talked to at the station shortly before Pease noticed her car was stolen. Nguyen asked the men why they had returned, and they replied that they needed gas. As he talked to them, he took the keys out of the ignition. Then he offered the men water while Pease secretly called 911.

Sensing that they had made a critical mistake in returning to the scene of the crime, the chumps fled on foot. Nguyen followed them through a back alley and was soon joined by two Escambia County sheriff's deputies and a police dog. The cops caught one suspect in some brush and the other across the street from the station. The crooks were jailed on grand theft auto and resisting-arrest charges.

Said Pease, "I'm glad my car was low on gas." And it helped that the suspects were low on common sense.

In a Word—Busted

How to make it really easy for the cops: Jot down all your crimes and criminal plans in your diary.

Police were called to investigate a report of a vehicle break-in in Stratford, Ontario, Canada, in 2002. The owner of the car said she saw a woman trying to steal her vehicle. After screaming at the would-be thief, the owner ran back into her house and called the cops.

When they arrived, the police followed fresh footprints in the snow from the crime scene to an apartment where a woman answered the door in her pajamas. She invited the officers in and told them to make themselves comfortable while she went into her bedroom and got dressed. While they waited for her to change, the cops noticed an open diary on the kitchen table. So they began reading it.

To their amazement, the entry for the day included plans to steal a vehicle: "Guess I'll get ready to see what kind of car I can grab today. Hopefully one with lots of gas and extra cash for gas."

In the next entry, written shortly before the officers arrived, the woman wrote in her diary, "Well, so much for that idea. I got caught getting out of a woman's truck and she freaked."

The culprit was arrested, and the diary was confiscated as evidence.

Pretty Bold—and Stupid

A car thief was either supremely confident or supremely stupid. You be the judge.

In 2006, a Clarion County, Pennsylvania, woman went to apply for a job as a clerk at a state police barracks. She filled out the forms and then was fingerprinted, as all applicants were. Imagine the cops' surprise when a swift background check of the woman revealed that there was an outstanding warrant against her for stealing an auto in Georgia.

Police arrested the woman from Strattanville, Pennsylvania, while she was waiting for her job interview. Then they went to the parking lot and found that the car she had driven to the state police barracks was indeed the one that had been reported stolen.

Lost Soul

A slow-witted carjacker didn't get far after he asked directions. For a criminal, this was dumb, because he was telling someone else his destination. Even dumber, he asked for directions from a television news crew.

In 2008, newswoman Shannon O'Brien and cameraman Eric Walls of CBS affiliate WOIO-TV in Cleveland, Ohio, were doing a sidewalk report on bank problems when an SUV pulled up. The man on the passenger's side asked O'Brien for directions to a nearby bank. While the passenger was talking to her, she couldn't help but notice that the driver looked scared, was shaking his head vigorously to her, and signaling that he was being held at gunpoint.

When O'Brien backed away, the passenger ordered the driver to drive off. Suspecting that the passenger was a carjacker, the newswoman and her cameraman jumped into their own vehicle and began tailing the SUV. She called 911 and told the dispatcher that the news team was in hot pursuit of a possible carjacker. By pinpointing the direction and location of the SUV, O'Brien guided police to the vehicle.

When the cops stopped the vehicle, they rescued the driver and captured the carjacker, who had a fully loaded gun in the front seat. He was charged with aggravated robbery and tossed in jail, where it was impossible for him to get lost.

Hot Pants

There was absolutely no doubt that the dimwit who robbed an Orlando, Florida, bank in 2006 was an amateur. When he walked into the Centura Bank, he shouted, "I'm holding down the joint!"

Huh? He didn't know that the proper way to announce that you're robbing a bank is to yell, "I'm holding *up* the joint!"

There was something else he didn't know—that banks use dye packs to foil bandits nonviolently. Whenever possible during a holdup, a teller puts one of these ignitable devices in the stack of money before turning the loot over to a robber. Within the dye pack is a small radio receiver that picks up a signal sent by a transmitter at the bank door. This activates a timer that causes the pack to explode in a shower of red ink intended to permanently stain the stolen money and the robber's hands.

Most self-respecting bank robbers know this, but not this dunderhead.

After botching his announcement that he was robbing the bank, he forced a teller to give him stacks of money. Because he forgot to bring something to carry the loot in, he stuffed the bills into his waistband. With so much money, he had to push the bills down into his underwear and out of view.

He quickly exited the bank and hustled down a busy street while being tailed by a bank employee. The robber didn't get far before the dye pack that was concealed in the loot exploded, covering him in red dye and smoldering his pants. Police spokesperson Sergeant Barbara Jones told the *Orlando Sentinel*, "Witnesses said they could see smoke coming out of his pants." Talk about burning a hole in your pocket.

Officers had no trouble picking out the suspect in the crowd. His pained expression and the bright red dye on his hands and the front of his pants were dead giveaways. The robber, who was identified by bank employees and security-camera footage, was taken to police headquarters for questioning. After he was charged with attempted robbery, he walked gingerly to a waiting ambulance with the help of police officers and firefighters. He was taken to the hospital for treatment of his burned and dyed groin. Adding to his pain and embarrassment, no one at the hospital knew how to remove the red dye from his body.

Hard to See Beyond His Nose

A man who planned to rob a bank had thought of almost everything. He cut out a large square of checkered cloth for his hood so no one could identify him. He bought white cloth gardening gloves so he wouldn't leave any fingerprints. He had a blue plastic shopping bag so he could carry all the loot.

When it came time to pull off the heist in 2003, he arrived outside the Oak Valley Community Bank in Modesto, California. He put on his gloves, draped the cloth over his head to hide his face, secured it with a hat, and . . . uh-oh. He had forgotten one small detail: to cut out eyeholes in his hood so he could see.

Because he was already at the bank, he figured he might as well rob it anyway. Picture a man whose face is completely covered in a checkered cloth hood held on by a baseball cap. He's wearing white gloves, a long-sleeved pink shirt, and tight faded blue jeans. And let's not forget the shopping bag.

Without the eyeholes, the robber had to slightly lift the hood's front corner so he could see where he was walking. But he couldn't lift the cloth too high without revealing his face. As a result, he was forced to walk with a noticeable shuffle, trying not to bump into anything or anyone.

Why nobody stopped him, who knows? Somehow he muddled up to the teller and demanded money. The teller gave him cash, which the crook stuffed in his shopping bag. Then he turned around and shuffled toward the door, all the while carefully holding up the front corner of his hood.

He forgot which side the front door hinges were on. The klutz slammed right into the steel door frame, banging his head hard enough to knock his hat off. That caused the hood to slip up, giving witnesses a good look at his face. Somewhat dazed by the impact, he backed up, adjusted his hood, and then staggered out the door. He got into a car that was driven by an accomplice and sped off.

Within a few days, the suspect brazenly—or perhaps stupidly—returned to the bank's neighborhood, where he was spotted by one of the witnesses, who immediately called the police. Moments later, the crook was booked at the Stanislaus County Men's Jail on a bank robbery charge.

The Good and the Bad

It was one of those good day/bad days for a bumbling bank robber.

The good: In 2002, the crook walked into a Wachovia Bank in North Miami Beach, Florida. As he approached the teller, he pulled a handgun out of his pocket and pointed it at her. He demanded that she fill up a bag with money. The teller did as she was told and gave him $16,000.

The bad: As he rushed for the exit, he stuffed the gun into his waistband, accidentally firing it into his pants, scaring everyone in the bank, especially him.

The good: The bullet missed him, and he scurried out of the bank.

The bad: When he ran into the street, he was struck by a van delivering school lunches in the area. Dazed and bleeding, he was pulled out from underneath the van. He lost two gold front teeth, his gun, and hat.

The good: He managed to stumble a short distance to a waiting getaway car driven by a woman and made his escape.

The bad: His two gold teeth, gun, and hat were left lying in the street—all crucial evidence that could link him to the crime.

The really bad: The FBI later matched DNA from the teeth with the robber's DNA file, proving he had been in the bank.

The really, really bad: A few days after the robbery, he was arrested at a Miami hotel, where agents found a sock full of money stuffed into his trousers. The serial numbers from the recovered money matched the bills taken from the bank.

The really, really, really bad: In 2003 he was convicted of bank robbery and faced up to life imprisonment.

Missed the Bus

For a not-so-bright woman, the bank heist went off without a hitch. However, the getaway didn't. That's because she was caught while waiting for the bus.

In 2008, this birdbrain went up to a teller at a Wachovia Bank in Sandy Springs, Georgia, and demanded money. Even though the woman didn't show any weapon, the teller didn't want to take any chances and gave her a bag of cash.

It seemed way too easy. It was. What the bandit didn't know was that the teller had put a dye pack in with the money. So, as the woman ran across a parking lot toward a Quiznos restaurant, the dye pack exploded, spraying her and the money in bright orange dye.

She ran next door to a Publix Super Market and made a beeline for the bathroom, where she ditched her dye-covered clothes and the money. Having brought other clothes with her, she quickly changed, calmly walked to nearby bus stop, and waited for a bus to take her home.

But by this time, one of the police officers who had been combing the area for suspects spotted the woman, who matched the description of the robber. He arrested her, and when she was taken to the police station, she confessed.

When asked what made her think she could escape on public transportation, the robber revealed that she had used the bus as her getaway vehicle two weeks earlier after she had robbed a Wachovia branch bank in DeKalb County.

"That just wasn't too bright," police spokesman Lieutenant Steve Rose told the *Atlanta Journal Constitution*. The woman was charged with two counts of robbery.

The Sandy Springs bank branch was no stranger to bumbling bandits, Rose said. "Another lady blew a robbery at the same place." In that crime, which happened in 2006, the would-be robber put a black bag and a white bag on the counter, and had the teller load all the money into the white bag. Rose said, "She took off with the black bag."

Name That Loser

It's never a good idea to rob a bank if you leave behind your real name and address.

A blockhead who planned to rob a bank had it all figured out. But when he walked into the bank in 2007, he didn't have any paper on which to write his holdup note. So he came up with a brainless idea: He wrote the note on the back of one of his own checks.

The dummy thought he was clever because he tried to cover up his name on the check by crossing it out with a pen. Then he handed the note to a teller at the Bank of the West in Englewood, Colorado.

The robber was feeling pretty good about himself as he fled the bank after the teller gave him $5,000 . But when the FBI was called in and looked at the demand note, they easily determined who the culprit was. "We could still make out his name even though he blacked it out," FBI agent Rene VonderHaar said. Surveillance video showed the bandit matched the suspect's description.

Knowing the jig was up, the robber turned himself in to federal authorities.

■　■　■

In 2008 in McAllen, Texas, a woman scrawled a holdup message on the back of a completed food-stamp application. Then she walked into a Capital One Bank and handed the teller the threatening note, forgetting that on the other side of the paper she had printed her real name and address.

After the teller gave her some money, the robber fled the scene. When the bank manager turned over the holdup note and saw the filled-out application, he showed it to the police. The cops tracked down the bandit at her address and arrested her within two hours of the robbery.

■ ■ ■

A lazybones decided to rob a bank in Fort Worth, Texas, in 2003. At home, he put a large piece of metal in a bag, which he planned to use to scare the teller into thinking it was a bomb. Then he grabbed a piece of paper and wrote out a threatening note for the teller, saying that he had a bomb and to give him all the money.

When he finished jotting the message, he discovered that he had written it on the back of a neatly typed job résumé that he had filled out earlier. He didn't want to go through all the trouble of finding a fresh sheet of paper and writing his holdup note over again. He didn't have time. After all, he had a bank to rob. So the dumbbell taped pieces of black construction paper over the information on the front side of the résumé.

Then he hurried down to the Wells Fargo Bank, put on a mask, and rushed up to a counter, where he plunked down two big brown paper bags and handed the teller his holdup note. The note said there was a bomb in one bag, and that it would go off if the teller didn't fill the other bag, which was empty, with money.

The teller stuffed the empty bag with two thousand dollars in small bills. Pleased with his haul, the robber grabbed both bags and scooted out the door. He forgot one thing—the holdup note.

When police arrived, they peeled off the taped black construction paper from the other side of the note and . . . voilá! . . . found their man's résumé. It was nicely done, complete with all the information the cops needed—name, address, phone number, and employment record.

When captured at his house, the crook presumably hadn't listed *bank robber* as one of his jobs.

Double Trouble

A bad guy who robbed a bank decided that because he got away with it once, he could get away with it twice. Just two weeks later, he went back to the same bank and tried to rob it again. The problem was that on his second attempt, the dunderhead wore the exact same outfit that he had the first time. And he did little to hide his identity.

Was there any doubt that the bank employees recognized him?

For his first robbery, in February 2008, the thief donned a black-and-gray hooded ski jacket and jeans. He also wore a baseball cap under a winter knit cap. He entered the Sovereign Bank in Plaistow, New Hampshire, went up to the teller, and demanded cash. The teller handed over an undisclosed amount of money, and the bandit hurried out of the bank and jumped into a black truck. The heist was caught on surveillance cameras.

Just two weeks later, he made a return engagement. The moment he stepped inside the bank, employees—whose memories were still fresh from the earlier robbery— recognized him instantly because he was wearing the exact same outfit.

This time when he ordered the teller to give him money, the teller refused. If the bandit had a gun, he didn't show it. Instead he fled the building and got into his black truck. But the bank manager had already called 911.

When police captured him, the suspect confessed to robbing three other banks. Wearing the same clothes wasn't the only reason why the employees at the Sovereign Bank recognized him. He had been one of their regular customers.

So Much for Keeping a Low Profile

A bank robber carried out his crime with class—and stupidity. That's because he used an attention-grabbing stretch limousine for his getaway car.

One day in 2007, the 31-year-old San Francisco man hired a limo to take him from his studio, where he worked as a personal trainer, to the airport. On the way there, he directed the driver to a Bank of America branch. He walked into the bank, told two tellers that he had a handgun, and robbed them of $5,000.

A witness spotted the robber get into the limo and leave. Police were alerted and had no difficulty finding the vehicle and pulling it over a few blocks away from the bank. They arrested him on the spot.

"It's a stretch limousine—not exactly the most discreet getaway vehicle," Police Inspector Dan Gardner told the *San Francisco Chronicle*. The driver, he added, "got stiffed," meaning the fool didn't pay him.

"It's just one of those things," the driver, Cornelius Weekley, owner of My Way Limo, told the newspaper. He said he had driven for the man about eight times, usually for socializing and such occasions as New Year's Eve. "But that was always in the evening when the banks are closed," Weekley said. "I thought he was pretty successful, but you never know." In an understatement, he said that chauffeuring around a bank robber "was a big surprise."

The chump, who earned a free ride to jail, pleaded guilty to robbery and was sentenced to a year in the county jail and five years' probation.

Bank Crank

A slow-witted gunman who tried to rob a bank before it opened wound up getting locked inside, unable to get out.

In 2006 in San Gabriel, California, an employee for the Bank of the West arrived in the parking lot about 8:30 A.M. to prepare to open it when she was confronted by a gunman who forced her inside.

Realizing he was a few peas short of a casserole, the woman told him she had to deactivate the bank alarm or else the police would arrive. He agreed, but actually she set the alarm to notify the police. The robber asked if she could open the vault. She said no, because it required a second worker who was scheduled to be there in five or ten minutes.

The woman looked out a window and saw the police had arrived, but the robber still had no idea they were coming. While waiting for the second employee, the robber told the woman to "go outside and look around and act as though everything is normal." She thought that was an excellent idea. She went outside—and then locked the bank door with her keys and ran over to the officers.

When it finally dawned on the gunman that he had been bamboozled, he refused to come out of the bank for several hours. Then he got hungry and tired and finally gave himself up.

A Wrapper of a Case

It's hard to know what's worse—being a lamebrain or a litterbug. A would-be bank robber was caught because he was both.

Late one night in 2003 in the little town of Marked Tree, Arkansas, the nitwit smashed the glass door of a bank and went inside. Without a mask or any other gear to hide his identity, he looked directly at the bank's security cameras. He also triggered an alarm.

When he realized that all the money was in the vault because the bank was closed, he stole a clock radio. On his way out, he stuffed his pockets with wrapped candy that was kept in bowls for customers to enjoy. As he left the bank, he ate the candy, carelessly tossing the wrappers on the sidewalk.

When police examined the crime scene, they spotted a trail of discarded candy wrappers. So they followed it to the burglar's home in a nearby trailer park. He was arrested and charged with robbery.

"It's a classic," said Patrolman Jerry Lung of the Marked Tree Police Department. "It was almost like he wanted to be caught."

The name of the candy couldn't have been more appropriate: "Dum Dums."

Caught Holding the Bag

A bank robbery was thwarted when a bungling culprit accidentally showed police his holdup note.

One afternoon in 2004, police in Hillsborough, North Carolina, received a call that a suspicious person with a book bag came into the BB&T Bank, stayed about 15 minutes, and left without approaching any teller. To the employees, it seemed like he was casing the place.

Captain Dexter Davis and Sergeant Brad Whitted drove to the bank. Before they arrived, the suspect returned to the bank and started walking toward a teller's window. But then he spotted the cops, so he turned around and headed for the front door.

Seeing that the man matched the description of the suspicious character, Davis stopped him and asked to see some identification. The guy produced several cards that had his name on them. He seemed nervous and asked why the officer had stopped him.

"I asked if he had a weapon," Davis recalled during an interview with the *Herald-Sun* of Durham. "He pulled his book bag off his shoulders, opened the bag, and held it open to me. I looked down and there was a note that said, 'I want ten thousand dollars in one-hundred-dollar bills. Don't push no buttons, or I'll shoot you.'"

The would-be robber had assumed that his holdup note was safely tucked away. Somehow, when he swung the book bag off his shoulder and opened it up, the note slipped into perfect position so that it was lying flat in the backpack and easy to read when Davis looked inside.

"I thought, 'What a dummy!'" Davis recalled. "I even showed it to Sergeant Whitted. I almost chuckled when I saw that note. I was looking for a weapon, but here was this note with nice large letters."

When asked about the note, the dummy said, "'It ain't mine,'"

Davis recalled. The officer put down the bag and handcuffed him. "We patted him down and at that point, a butcher knife fell out of his britches," Davis said. The blade of the knife was at least 10 inches long and had a sharp point.

Although the Hillsborough police didn't charge him with any crimes, because he hadn't actually attempted to rob the bank, he was turned over to the Durham Police Department and the FBI, because he was wanted in connection with an attempted robbery of the Central Carolina Bank.

In that other case, the same bandit had handed a teller a note demanding a specific amount of money in specific denominations. When the teller told him she didn't have the money in those denominations, he had become angry and had stormed out of the bank.

Just a Minute Too Late

A would-be bank robber picked the wrong time to attempt his crime.

The featherbrain drove to the parking lot of the Citizens & Northern Bank in Liberty, Pennsylvania, at 11:40 A.M. and sat in his car for 21 minutes one day in 2008. When he finally got up the nerve to rob it, he donned an orange ski mask, pulled out his shotgun, and ran to the entrance of the bank, but the doors were locked and the bank had closed.

It was a Thursday, and he failed to notice that on Thursdays, the bank closed at noon because it was open for longer hours on Friday. He had reached the front door at 12:01 P.M..—one minute late. After shaking the front door, he attracted the attention of the employees inside, who immediately called the police. They gave a good description of the shotgun-toting man in the orange mask. They also reported that he sped off in a green Subaru Forester and gave the police the license plate number.

Police soon captured him. They charged him with a first-degree felony count of attempted robbery and a misdemeanor count of possessing an instrument of crime.

Crime Doesn't Pay

A woman suspected of robbing a bank turned herself in to the police—because she wanted to claim the $2,500 reward for her arrest!

In 2007, a Bank of America branch in Jacksonville, North Carolina, was robbed by a woman. She arrived at the bank in a taxi, told tellers that she had a firearm, and left with an undisclosed amount of money in the same cab. According to the police, the driver didn't know that his fare was a bank robber.

Bank security-camera images, eyewitness accounts, and a search of the police database helped identify the suspect. But the cops couldn't find her. So a $2,500 reward was offered by Crime Stoppers of Onslow County for information leading to the arrest of the suspect.

A 10-day search came to an end when the 45-year-old woman entered the lobby of the Onslow County Sheriff's Department a few minutes past midnight and turned herself in to the night dispatcher. But then she demanded the reward for her arrest. As stunned deputies listened to her bizarre claim, she told them that she wanted the money to go to her friend, who had accompanied her to the station. After all, what are friends for if not to give them money?

Actually, the friend could have used the money—to pay the suspect's bail.

Tooting His Own Horn

A bank robber who was hoping to win a prize on a talk-radio show bragged about his unsolved crime—and was soon arrested.

In September 2004, DJ Drex's morning show on Chicago's WKSC-FM (103.5) featured callers confessing to various misdeeds such as committing road rage or stealing items at work. But a caller who wanted to be known simply as "D" volunteered a shocking admission—that he and five others had pulled off the robbery of a TCF Bank in

South Chicago Heights. He gave specific details of the crime, which had gone unsolved for five months. He revealed that an employee had been part of the heist and that the robbers went into the bank vault and, while avoiding the dye packs, made off with $81,000.

"So . . . we set everything up," he boasted on the air. "We planned it out. Turned my house into a bank for like weeks." He even bragged about buying himself an expensive wallet to carry around some of the stolen loot. "D" added that his fellow robbers were also spending their ill-gotten gains on high-priced clothes and other glitzy items.

It just so happened that a TCF employee who was driving to work the morning of the broadcast heard "D's" boastful tale on DJ Drex's show. Realizing that "D" was talking about the April holdup of her bank, she called authorities.

FBI agents went to the radio station, which had a tape of the call. The station also turned over a cell phone number registered to the suspect. The feds arrested him later that day and put out warrants for the others involved in the robbery.

FBI officials and prosecutors said that "D's" bragging was the break they needed. Authorities didn't have a good description of the robbers, because the employees had been tied up. "As a result we had no leads until one of the individuals in the robbery called 103.5," Assistant U.S.

Attorney Terra Brown said. "The details he provided were incredibly helpful in moving this investigation forward."

After his arrest, "D" told the FBI he made the call hoping to win a prize for the best confession of the day on the show. As far as the FBI was concerned, this loser was a winner for helping them solve the case.

Psst, Look Over Your Shoulder

A blockhead was so intent on robbing a bank that when he walked up to the teller, he was clueless that the person standing right behind him in line was a police officer in uniform.

On New Year's Eve 2007, this dum-dum walked into the Mt. Washington Bank in Boston and immediately drew suspicion because he was wearing white gloves, an oversize hooded parka, and a scarf that covered his face. Employees alerted Officer Kamau Pritchard, who was working security at the bank.

Hurrying from a back room where he had been on a break, Pritchard cut in line so he was right behind the man. Just then the clueless crook passed a note to a teller demanding large bills and no "funny money." The officer later told the *Boston Globe*, "He didn't realize I was behind him. He was focused on actually getting the money. The teller stalled before handing over a stack of bills. Then [the teller] starts saying, 'He's trying to rob me.'"

As the robber turned around, Pritchard drew his service revolver and arrested him. The criminal, who did not have a gun, was charged with unarmed bank robbery.

Stopover

After robbing a bank, the crook hopped into his getaway car and discovered that he was low on gas and out of cigarettes. So what did the birdbrain do? He stopped at a service station for fuel and some smokes—just long enough for the cops to find him.

The robber entered a bank in Bayonet Point, Florida, one day in 2002. He gave the teller a note that said, "I have a gun, give me all the money." He walked out with an undisclosed amount of cash, got in a white Buick Century sedan, and drove west. So far, so good. But rather than get as far away as possible, he stopped at a nearby store about fifteen minutes after bank employees reported the crime.

He asked the clerk for a pack of cigarettes and five dollars' worth of gas. While inside, it dawned on him that stopping there was a bad idea. Maybe it was because he saw the police cruiser across the street.

"He was very nervous. He kept looking out the window at the cop car," the clerk recalled.

A Pasco County sheriff's deputy in the cruiser spotted the bandit's vehicle, which matched the description of the robber's getaway car. The deputy called for backup units and approached the store. Meanwhile, inside the Circle K, the crook turned to leave without his cigarettes until the clerk reminded him the pack was still on the counter.

He went back for the cigarettes, and by the time he pushed open the door, the deputy was standing about 15 feet away with his gun drawn. The deputy approached the store and yelled for the robber to get down on the ground.

Instead of dropping to the ground, the crook shouted, "I didn't do anything!" Hard to believe, especially when he took off running behind the station. The deputy and backup units pursued him. After a 10-minute foot chase, deputies caught him in a swampy area about a quarter mile from the store.

The robber, who had a lengthy criminal record, was charged with armed robbery and auto theft, because the getaway car had been reported stolen. Too bad for him that he didn't plan ahead and fill up his car and buy his cigarettes before robbing the bank.

Pushing the Wrong Buttons

A purse snatcher accidentally turned on a stolen cell phone, unwittingly leading police right to him.

The crook walked into a woman's shelter in Hartford, Connecticut, one day in 2002 pretending to show up for a business appointment. But when workers turned their backs, he took the purse belonging to the shelter's executive director and fled. He had planned to use stolen credit cards in the purse to buy clothes at a nearby store.

When the police were called to the shelter, they learned that among the items in the purse was the director's cell phone. The cops wondered if the thief would be so dumb that he would answer the phone. It was worth a try, because the typical criminal is often one doughnut short of a dozen. Officer Robert Russell used his own cell phone to call the number—and couldn't believe his luck.

The thief started to answer the phone, but then thought better of it. His problem was he didn't know how to stop the darn phone from ringing. He punched this button and that button until he thought he had turned it off. But he hadn't. In fact, he had answered the call and left it on, so Russell could hear what he was doing. The officer could tell that the crook was in a store, shopping for clothes.

"He was saying things like, 'I'd like that in yellow' and 'I'll need some pants to go along with that,'" Russell later told the *Hartford Courant*. "So we knew he must've gone into some store close by."

Keeping his own phone to his ear, Russell hopped into his squad car and headed for a nearby shopping area. He kept listening for the sounds coming over the cell phone and stopped at four stores. When he walked into the Above Us clothing store, he noticed that the music in the shop matched the music coming over his cell phone. "I was like, 'Okay, he's in here,'" Russell recalled. "And sure enough, I saw a guy who fit his description behind a rack of clothes."

Russell said he looked right at the suspect, who tried to charge past him. Unsure if the man had a weapon, the officer doused him with pepper spray. The thief was charged with sixth-degree larceny, interfering with a police officer, criminal impersonation, breach of peace, and criminal mischief.

Russell, a 19-year veteran of the force, said it wasn't too tough to catch the thief. "I've had a few names in my book of dumb criminals," the officer told the newspaper, "but this guy goes right to the top."

Blazing a Trail

The dumber the crook, the easier it is to solve the case.

Take, for example, the noodlehead who tried to steal a five-thousand-dollar commercial paint sprayer. The piece of equipment had been used by a contract painting crew that was working on a building in Cedar Grove, Florida, in 2003. When the men, who had been staying at a motel for the weeklong job, were getting ready to leave for work early one morning, they discovered the sprayer was missing from their trailer in the parking lot.

Police had no trouble solving the case. That's because the sprayer sometimes dripped for days after being turned off. Paint had leaked onto the sprayer's wheels, so when the thief took it off the trailer and wheeled it away the night before, it left a 700-foot trail of ivory-colored paint on the blacktop, which led right to the crook's home!

The cops recovered the sprayer from his yard and obtained an arrest warrant on charges of burglary and grand theft.

What a Fuel-ish Thing to Do

One fall night in 2005, a white van pulled up to a Swifty gas station in Muncie, Indiana, even though the station was closed. It was exactly what a sneaky crook wanted.

When the station manager arrived early the next morning, he saw that the van was parked directly over one of his underground storage tanks. Seeing that a hose was connected from a tank opening to the vehicle, the manager called the police.

When the cops arrived, they found a man asleep in the van while a battery-operated pump was sucking gasoline out of the underground tank and into a 55-gallon container that he had installed in the back of the van. The cops arrested the man and charged him with theft.

"That's a lot of gas," Police Chief Joe Winkle said. "I'm sure he felt like this would be a pretty good heist." With regular unleaded at the station selling for $2.67 at the time, the tank would have held nearly $150 worth of gas.

Pumping the fuel out of the storage tank took so long that the thief fell asleep sometime during the night. "He may have just got tired trying to fill that large drum up with gasoline," said Winkle. "If he had stayed awake, he probably would have gotten away with the theft. Now he'll have plenty of time to sleep—in jail."

No Job for Him

Either because he was bold or dumb, a thief applied for a job at the same place he had robbed two days earlier.

The knucklehead sought work at JB Construction in Stillwater,

Oklahoma, in 2003. When he was ushered into the office for a job interview, several employees recognized him as the man caught on a surveillance camera stealing a one-hundred-dollar laser level from the business and a thousand dollars' worth of CDs from an employee's car 48 hours earlier.

"The business owner called and said, 'I think the thief is here filling out a job application,'" Payne County sheriff's deputy Sammie Dawson told the Associated Press. Police raced down to the construction office and arrested the dolt right in the middle of his job interview.

In jail, he confessed. "When he went out there to apply for the job a few days earlier, he didn't see anyone around, and the place was unlocked," Payne County Undersheriff Kenneth Willerton told reporters. "So he just helped himself to some items and left."

Not realizing his theft had been videotaped, the thief returned two days later, hoping to land a job. Needless to say, he didn't get it.

Hey, Dad, Aren't You Forgetting Something?

A shoplifter looking to make a quick getaway from a supermarket left behind a crucial piece of evidence—his 12-year-old son.

In the Dutch town of Kerkrade in 2008, the 45-year-old thief brought his son with him to the supermarket and tried to shoplift a package of meat. When he was spotted by an employee, the culprit dashed toward his car with the worker in hot pursuit. The worker flung himself onto the hood of the thief's car to thwart the escape, but the shoplifter batted him away, jumped in the car, and sped off. In his haste, he forgot his son.

After the boy gave police his home phone number, police contacted the dimwit, but he refused to return to get his son. The man told officers to call the youngster's mother instead. The thief, who didn't exactly become a role model for his son, later turned himself in.

Christmastime Crime

A holiday thief proved he wasn't one of the brightest bulbs on the Christmas tree.

Shortly before the Christmas holiday in 2007, the owner of the Montana Wreaths & Pink Grizzly Christmas Store in Missoula, Montana, reported a theft after he saw a man walking with a shopping cart full of stolen holiday decorations that he recognized came from the store.

The owner later saw two of his artificial Christmas trees in the yard of a mobile home a few blocks from his shop. When he went to investigate, he discovered stacks of wreaths from his store in the entryway, so he called the police.

Confronted by a sheriff's deputy, the suspect denied breaking into the store. He claimed that he had made all the wreaths at his home after finding wreath-making supplies that had been abandoned near the store.

He was charged with felony burglary because his story simply wasn't believable. That's because the red and yellow price tags from the Pink Grizzly were still attached to the artificial Christmas trees and some of the wreaths.

What a Card

A thief who stole a golf bag filled with hundreds of dollars' worth of clubs couldn't believe his luck when he found a restaurant gift card inside. Not only could he sell the stolen clubs at various pawnshops, but he would be eating for free, too, or so he thought.

In 2008, Joey Polychronis, 15, of Salt Lake City, set his golf bag outside the Mountain Dell Golf Course clubhouse and went inside to pay his greens fee. That's when the thief ran off with the clubs. Joey assumed he would never see them again. Ah, but one should never underestimate the stupidity of a crook.

In the golf bag, Joey had a $25 gift card to any of three Squatters Brew Pubs, which were owned by his father, Jeff Polychronis. Joey had planned to give the card later to a family friend as a present. Figuring that the thief might be dumb enough to use the card, Jeff alerted the managers of his restaurants to be on the lookout for the gift card.

One of the restaurant managers checked his computer files and discovered the card had been used on the night of the theft. Because there was still seven dollars left on the card, Jeff hoped the thief would return. The owner sent an e-mail to his staff offering a cash reward to any employee who caught the culprit if he tried to use the card again.

Sure enough, the thief returned two days later, presented the card to a server, and asked how much value the card had left on it. Once she realized that it was the stolen card, she stalled him, telling him to wait a few minutes, because the computers were down. While he was waiting, she called the Salt Lake City police, who showed up at the restaurant and arrested him. The thief eventually confessed, and most of the golf clubs were recovered from area pawnshops. It's unlikely that once he got out of jail, he would ever again set foot in a Squatters restaurant.

When Things Don't Go According to Plan

Would-be thieves in Hillsborough, North Carolina, in 2006 thought it would be a snap to steal an ATM.

They mounted an unattended backhoe from a nearby construction project and drove it to a SunTrust ATM at a shopping center. The crooks positioned a stolen Chevrolet S10 pickup truck next to the ATM. Using the heavy equipment, the backhoe operator pried the ATM from its foundation. But when he tried to load the ATM into the bed of the truck, the vehicle, like the thieves' hearts, sank.

The overwhelming weight of the cash machine was too much for the small vehicle. The truck collapsed and couldn't move. Giving up on their scheme, the crooks had to leave on foot.

When police arrived, they found the abandoned ATM, backhoe, and small-bodied pickup. There's no telling what the culprits felt after their failed attempt.

Taking the Wrong Track

Can you think of a dumber thing to steal than a portable tracking device?

Well, some guy who was a few Cheerios shy of a full bowl did just that in Janesville, Wisconsin. When he snatched the device, it automatically alerted the police and gave them the dummy's location.

At the time in this county, low-risk, nonviolent inmates were sent home with electronic tracking equipment. These offenders placed a tracking device in their home and wore a small transmitter on their ankle. If they wandered more than 100 feet from their tracking device, the county jail was alerted. Each battery-powered device had a built-in global positioning system that transmitted its location back to the jail through the Internet. The jail usually had five to eight inmates on home detention at any one time while officials checked their whereabouts on a computerized map.

In 2003, one of the tracking devices was issued to a Janesville woman who was on home detention for a drunken-driving conviction. She had put the device on the grass outside her home.

Minutes later, a thief walked by and spotted the $2,500 device. He just couldn't help himself. He swiped it. As soon as he left the yard, the jail received an alert that the woman's tracking device had left her home zone. She called the jail and reported that it had been stolen.

Correctional Officer Thomas Roth, who ran the home-detention program, was able to track the device on his home computer. A trail of electronic dots on the monitor showed exactly where the device was traveling and where it stopped. Police were dispatched to that location and arrested the featherbrain on a charge of felony theft.

Said Roth, "He apparently didn't know what he had, because he would be awfully stupid to steal a tracking device."

Counterfeiters and Forgers

A Prickly Situation

Two suspects fleeing from the police discovered, to their everlasting discomfort, that the best place to hide from the law is not in a patch of prickly cactus.

A woman tried to pass a forged check at a business in Mesa, Arizona, in 2008. A store employee became suspicious and called the police. As a squad car pulled into the parking lot, the woman jumped into the passenger side of the getaway car driven by her male accomplice.

He hit the gas and took off as police pursued them in cruisers and also in a helicopter. The car ran through red lights and crossed the center line into oncoming traffic, causing several vehicles to skid to a stop to avoid being hit head-on. The car sped through Mesa until the road ended.

That didn't stop the couple. They attempted to drive off-road into the desert, which wasn't too smart, because the car was designed to ride on streets. Bouncing and swerving in the rocky desert, the vehicle eventually became stuck and disabled on the Salt River Reservation.

The couple bailed out and ran deeper into the desert—and smack into a patch of nasty cholla cactus. Brushing against the cactus, the man and woman were soon in agony as the plants' sharp, barbed needles became embedded in their skin. When the Salt River Police Department officers finally captured them, the suspects looked like human pincushions.

They were arrested and taken to Banner Desert Medical Center for treatment. "I am so stupid," the guy said through tears as hospital workers plucked the cactus spines from his body. "This is what I get for trying to run from the police."

Way Too Much

A guy who forged a check got caught because he was way too greedy—billions of dollars too greedy.

The numbskull showed up at the Chase Bank in Fort Worth, Texas, one day in 2008 and presented tellers with a check made out for $360 billion. (That's 36 followed by ten zeros.) Because that's a lot more money than even the richest person in America has, bank employees became suspicious. They phoned the account holder—the woman who allegedly wrote out the check—and asked if she indeed had made out a check for $360 billion. Since the balance in her checking account was closer to $360 than it was to $360 billion, she told the bank that the check was a phony. She added that the forger was her daughter's boyfriend, and he did not have permission to cash any check of hers.

Employees then called the police, who arrested the man on a fraud charge. According to the *Fort Worth Star-Telegram*, when the forger was in the patrol car, he told police that his girlfriend's mother had given him the check to help him start his own record company. But on his way to jail, he was singing the blues.

Flawed Fraud

A crook who stole other people's identities and cashed hundreds of fake checks figured the only way to bail himself out of jail was to do what he knew best—pay with a counterfeit check.

The 54-year-old rascal from Sacramento, California, racked up more than $90,000 in fraudulent activity across four counties during a three-month period in 2005, according to Santa Cruz County prosecutors. He passed about 300 counterfeit checks in various cities throughout the state. He also committed online banking fraud and had several credit-card violations.

When he was finally arrested, he tried to make bail with a

counterfeit check. But the bail bondsman refused to accept the check, because he could tell it wasn't real. Later, the crook produced a second check so he was released. Once the man got out of jail, the bail bondsman discovered the check was a fake. How did he know? No bank in the world would print a set of checks with pictures of rabid puppies on them.

Officers caught up with the scam artist again, and this time they made it clear that if he wanted to post bail, it would be in cash—and for lots of money. Rather than go through a lengthy trial, he pleaded guilty to a variety of fraud and grand-theft charges and was given a sentence of seven to ten years in state prison.

He was living proof of where you'll end up if you commit check fraud after being caught committing check fraud.

Buying Trouble for Herself

A woman who was fired for misuse of a company credit card bought herself further legal problems when she paid court fines for three past criminal cases—by using the same credit card.

In 2007, the woman was fired from the Scotts Company in Clinton, Iowa, after the firm discovered that she had made several unauthorized payments using the credit-card number during her employment. She used the stolen number to pay more than $500 in vehicle repairs and to pay three court fines totaling nearly $700 for past legal problems.

She was arrested and charged with credit-card fraud, identity theft, and violation of probation. She pleaded guilty to second-degree theft and was sentenced to three years' probation.

Bogus Bills

A teenage counterfeiter thought it was so cool having a wad of bogus bills that he had his photo taken with his buddies. It didn't seem so cool after police used the photo to catch him.

The 17-year-old crook was passing counterfeit twenty- and hundred-dollar bills at the California State Fair in Sacramento in 2006. A fair vendor who was victimized by the counterfeiter told State Fair Police Chief Robert Craft that he remembered seeing the suspect carrying a photograph that looked like it had been taken at the fair's photo kiosk.

The cops went to the kiosk and examined copies of all the photos that had been taken there. They found what they were searching for—a picture taken of a young man with his friends holding lots of money.

Once the police knew exactly what the counterfeiter looked like, they kept an eye out for him, hoping he would return to the fair. He did come back and attempted to pass another counterfeit bill. The cops arrested him and found $400 in counterfeit bills in his pocket. The fool was charged with two felony counts of possessing or passing fake money.

"This is a dumb-crook thing," Craft told reporters. "You go in and have your picture taken and become a Ten Most Wanted here. Give me a break."

Turnabout Is Fair Play

There's nothing like giving crooks a taste of their own medicine.

In 2004, a counterfeiter entered a Wal-Mart store in suburban Cincinnati. He used the funny money to purchase about $400 worth of electronics, including a DVD player and several DVDs. After he left, an employee noticed the money was fake, but it was too late, because the punk was gone.

A short while later, his accomplice came into the same store with a receipt for the purchases and returned about $300 worth of the merchandise. She expected to receive real cash for her returned items, but the Wal-Mart clerk recognized the receipt as the one that belonged to the counterfeiter. Store management decided to teach the crooks a lesson. They gave the woman $300 in the same bogus bills that her comrade had given the store.

But management had used a counterfeit-detecting pen that left black marks on each bill, which would alert clerks at other stores that the money was fake. The woman didn't realize it until after she left.

Less than an hour later, the crooked couple returned to the store a third time, and had the gall to complain that the clerk had given them counterfeit money. The manager suggested that a call to the police was warranted. Before the cops arrived, however, the couple fled, victims of their own scam.

Funny Money Wasn't Funny

A Long Island man who was arrested for a string of traffic violations made matters worse when he tried to use counterfeit money to pay for his bail.

It just wasn't a good day for the 31-year-old crook. First, he was stopped for making an illegal left turn in front of a Suffolk County police sergeant. Then the man couldn't produce a driver's license or any other kind of identification. Reluctantly, he gave his real name, so the cop ran a check on him. It turned out that the man's license had been suspended a whopping 35 times. That was only the beginning. The officer cited him for unlicensed operation, too-dark tinted windows, and substandard tires.

The offender was hauled off to the police station. But rather than toss him in jail, the cops offered to release him if he could post a $500 bail, because all his violations were misdemeanors. The relieved man eagerly pulled out a stack of fifty-dollar bills. Unfortunately, he merely compounded his problems, because an officer noticed that one of the bills was counterfeit. The dumbbell paid the price for that fake bill. He was put behind bars and slapped with a felony charge of possessing counterfeit money.

Other Dumb Criminals

Police Posers

A 25-year-old oaf who posed as a cop picked the wrong motorist to pull over.

While driving on a highway on Long Island, New York, in 2007, the dope became irritated because he felt a car had cut him off. With flashing lights atop his Jeep Cherokee, he drove up next to the offending car and motioned for the driver to stop.

When the motorist refused, the angry fake cop wanted to scare the driver and chew him out, so he yelled through the open passenger's window, "Pull over! I'm a cop." Then the pretend policeman held up his fake badge. The driver wasn't impressed. In fact, the motorist scoffed at him and said, "That's not a real badge." The other driver flipped open a wallet and showed him a New York City Police Department badge and said, "*This* is a real badge."

Of all the people he could have tried to pull over, the pretend cop had attempted to stop a *real* cop, who happened to be an off-duty police detective. Imagine the odds of that! Now the tables were turned.

"Pull over!" ordered the real cop.

Instead, the impostor sped off, but the real cop tailed him, called 911, and then watched when more real police caught up to the fake cop and arrested him on charges of criminal impersonation and aggravated unlicensed operation of a motor vehicle.

■ ■ ■

A teenager who drove a vehicle equipped like an unmarked cop car thought it would be fun to pull people over for traffic stops.

His 2003 black Ford Crown Victoria had what many police cars have in Florida—sirens, a spotlight, flashing lights in the front grill, and a Florida State Troopers tag on the front bumper.

In 2008, the 17-year-old pretend cop from Tallahassee, Florida, spotted someone he wanted to stop and scare, so he turned on his siren and flashed his lights, causing the motorist to pull off to the side of the road.

What the teen hadn't counted on was someone else getting in on the act, someone like a real officer from the Tallahassee Police Department. The real cop was heading in the opposite direction when he saw what appeared to be a fellow officer in an unmarked car with its lights flashing at a traffic stop. Being a well-trained policeman, the cop turned his car around to back up a law-enforcement comrade.

Spotting the real cop, the impostor hopped back into his car and took off. Suspicious, the real officer drove after him and forced him to stop. Knowing the city didn't have any teenage cops on the force, the officer arrested the young man on a charge of impersonating a law-enforcement officer.

The Writing Is on the Wall

It wasn't all that difficult for police to nab an 18-year-old chucklehead who had vandalized a children's campsite building. The young man wrote his name on a wall at the scene of the crime.

According to authorities in Cheshire, England, in 2008 the teenager and a friend broke into the building in Adlington, Cheshire, and smashed plates and bowls and discharged fire extinguishers, spreading foam everywhere. Then he used a black marker to scrawl his real name on the wall, adding a final message to the building's owners, "THANKS FOR THE STAY."

Police found the culprit after they entered his name in a computer system. As if leaving his name at the crime scene wasn't stupid enough, when police tracked him down, he was wearing a T-shirt stolen from the campsite during the burglary.

He and his buddy pleaded guilty and were ordered to pay about $1,500 in compensation for the damage they caused.

Cheshire Police Inspector Gareth Woods told reporters, "This crime is up there with the dumbest of all in the criminal-league table. There are some pretty stupid criminals around, but to leave your own name at the scene of the crime takes the biscuit. The daftness of this lad certainly made our job a lot easier."

Attention Getter

A nitwit walked into a meeting with his probation officer wearing an expensive stolen watch—and walked out wearing handcuffs.

You would think that a guy who had a police record dating back 10 years would know better than to draw attention to his latest crime. Yet in 2007, in Santa Fe, New Mexico, this blockhead flashed a fancy Rolex watch—one valued at $2,500—during a regularly scheduled meeting with his probation officer who, naturally, became suspicious and called the police.

The cops went to the Probation and Parole Department and determined from markings on the watch that it was the same one stolen two days earlier during a home invasion. In that crime, a 61-year-old victim reported that three men forced their way into his house. They ransacked his bedroom and stole the watch along with the headset to a cordless phone that one of them snatched out of his hand.

When police questioned the suspect at the probation office, he claimed that the watch belonged to a friend who had left it at the suspect's house. They didn't believe him. Instead, they arrested him on a probation violation for possessing stolen property.

Santa Fe Deputy Police Chief Eric Wheeler told the *Santa Fe New Mexican*, "It goes back to that thought process that these guys aren't the sharpest tools in the shed."

The Name Game

Never lie to a police officer. It will only get you in more trouble. This lesson was not learned by a half-wit until he nearly got busted for a homicide he didn't commit.

In 2008, police in Sheboygan, Wisconsin, stopped a vehicle for improper registration. The driver gave police his license. Then the cops asked the passenger for his license. The passenger had collected a mound of unpaid traffic citations in another state and wasn't sure if there was a warrant out for his arrest, so he didn't want the police to know his true identity. He said he didn't have his license on him, so they asked him for his name.

He made one up. There are millions upon millions of names he could have chosen. Wouldn't you know, he picked a really bad name.

When the police ran a check on the name, it turned out to belong to someone who had an active felony warrant for vehicular homicide.

Just as the cops were about to arrest him on that serious charge, the passenger quickly gave police his real name. They weren't convinced, so they took him down to the station. There, they verified his true identity through photos and fingerprints and that he wasn't the suspect in the vehicular homicide.

He was still arrested on an obstruction charge.

Courting Trouble

A dummy found a surefire way to lose his court case—by beating up his attorney in front of the judge and jury.

In 2006, the 56-year-old defendant was on trial in Hibbing, Minnesota, after being charged with knifing two men during a dispute about their loud music. The incident was one of several in the thug's long criminal history, which included assault, armed robbery, and an armed escape from custody.

He didn't like the way his trial was going, saying he thought his court-appointed lawyer had "sabotaged" his defense, so he asked Judge James Florey for a new attorney. The judge said no. The brute was getting desperate, because he didn't want to go back to prison. So he came up with a new, more daring—and appalling—plan: He attempted to cause a mistrial so that he would have to be tried again or released.

After everyone returned from a break, he suddenly attacked his lawyer, public defender Mark Groettum, from behind, locking his arm around his neck and punching him in the face. A chair was knocked over, and both men ended up on the floor before the attacker was restrained. It all happened in front of the shocked jury, the judge, and others in the courtroom. Groettum suffered a cut lip, black eye, and bloody nose.

After the attack, Groettum told Judge Florey that, ethically, he could no longer be the defendant's attorney. Because Florey had already refused to let the defendant have another lawyer, the assailant was forced to represent himself. The judge also ordered him shackled and dressed in his orange jail suit for the rest of the trial. (Usually an inmate is given the right to wear street clothes during a trial so the jury is not biased by his or her appearance.)

The lout might not have liked the way his trial was going, but it went a lot worse after the attack. He was convicted and is serving 14 years at the Moose Lake State Prison. For the assault on the lawyer, the judge threw in another six months for contempt of court.

Hey, Batter, You're Out!

Two teenagers were having so much fun vandalizing the neighborhood that they failed to notice the squad car in the driveway or the sheriff's deputy on the porch watching them destroy a mailbox.

A Washington County, Oregon, sheriff's deputy was working on a case at a resident's home one winter evening in 2008 when he stepped onto the porch to use his cell phone. According to the newspaper *Oregonian*, he saw a Jeep Cherokee drive slowly down the road that fronted the house. As the vehicle moved toward the shoulder in front of the neighbor's home, the deputy heard what he assumed was the Jeep hitting its tires on the road's edge.

The Jeep kept coming and pulled over right in front of him. Then a young man in the front passenger seat leaned out the window and clobbered the mailbox with a wooden bat. Only then did the deputy realize that the teens had been battering mailboxes along the road. They had smashed three mailboxes—including the one right in front of him next to his patrol car. Somehow, the vandals had failed to notice him or his car.

The deputy got into his vehicle and pulled the Jeep over. Inside were four teenagers—the driver and the batter, both 18, and two kids riding in the back, including a 16-year-old exchange student from Germany who was bewildered by the whole thing.

The deputy ordered all four to sit on the ground in the cold December air while he searched them for weapons. The batter, who had thrown his club out the window and played dumb about wrecking the mailboxes, later confessed to the vandalism. He and the driver were charged with second-degree criminal mischief.

A Sorry Picture

Three dim teenagers who posed at a portrait studio bolted without paying the sitting fee. It never dawned on them that the ripped-off photographer had the full-color pictures that they had posed for, which he turned over to the police and the media.

Two girls and a boy stepped into Tony's Old Time Portrait Studio in Victoria, British Columbia, Canada, in 2008. It's a business where people can dress up in period costumes and have their picture taken. Owner Tony Bohanan and his staff spent more than 40 minutes dressing the teenagers in costumes befitting an Old West saloon, complete with mock pistols and hats. The trio were giggling, laughing, and whispering throughout the photo shoot.

After they changed back into their regular clothes and viewed their pictures on a computer monitor, the three took off running without paying the $84 sitting fee.

Stupidly, though, they left behind unmistakable evidence of their identities—the color photos that they had posed for. Bohanan turned the snapshots over to the police. Then he released the portraits to the media and asked the public to help identify the thieves. Once the photographic evidence made the news, the three sheepish teens turned themselves in to police. One of the girls paid the fee and apologized to Bohanan. The studio owner told the Victoria *Times Colonist*, "She said, 'I'm very sorry. We saw our pictures plastered all over the place, and it made me feel like a crook.'" The boy's father brought him to the studio to apologize to Bohanan, too. Then the other girl made an apology.

Although Victoria police said they could charge the three young offenders if Bohanan wanted, the 79-year-old owner declined, saying he didn't want to see the kids get in worse trouble. He was pleased that the three each came forward to say they were sorry. They were sorry, all right, in more ways than one.

Internet Idiocy

Why, oh why, would a crook want to blab about his crime all over the Internet? Maybe because his ego is bigger than his brain.

Here are some examples:

In February 2008, a 15-year-old Missouri boy went on the website gamefaqs.com, where video gamers get clues and chat with other gamers. He asked other posters if he should burn down a church.

The question was treated as a joke in bad taste, and was erased by the website's administrators. But the next morning on the website, posters asked him what had happened at the church. He replied that he had indeed torched a church and part of his school next door.

Some didn't believe him and asked for proof. So he posted camera-phone pictures of a large fire that destroyed Mission Hill Baptist Church in Palmyra, Missouri. The school was partially damaged. Among the most startling pictures was one he took of himself inside the church. He even directed posters to a local TV station's website, which had footage of the blaze, to show them what he had done.

Posters from Florida and Wisconsin who had seen the comments and pictures on the website were so alarmed they contacted the local TV station, WGEM, which in turn turned over the information to investigators who already knew the fire at Mission Hill had been set. Police arrested the boy and charged him with felony arson.

The following day, posters on the website expressed shock, wishing they had known it was not a joke, so they could have stopped it. As one person said, "At least this arsonist was dumb enough to make it easy for the cops to catch him."

■   ■   ■

It's no wonder two teenagers were charged with setting fires in suburban Washington. They bragged about the blazes on MySpace. com and even posted a video and photos of their crimes.

The 17-year-old schoolmates were involved in 17 fires in Montgomery County, Maryland, in 2006, fire officials said. The teens faced 22 charges, including two counts each of first-degree arson and four counts of second-degree arson.

Stores, vehicles, a bowling alley, and two school buses were set on fire over a four-month arson spree. Investigators received a tip to check out the online social networking site MySpace.com, where they found photos and descriptions of the firebugs' crimes. The teens even showed a video of themselves firebombing an abandoned airplane hangar.

"The significant thing is they posted on the Internet and bragged about the fires, and that allowed us to break the case," Fire Chief Thomas W. Carr Jr. told reporters. "They posted photos of these fires."

As dumbcriminal.com said later, "The only way the teens could have been dumber is if they posted routes to the scenes of the crimes from their houses on Mapquest and sold pieces of the burned debris on eBay and written songs about it and distributed them illegally on Napster."

Show-and-tell

A 21-year-old dumbbell became curious when he noticed two police officers demonstrating their squad-car computer equipment to children in a Detroit neighborhood in 1988. So he walked up to the officers and asked them to show him how their system worked.

The officers agreed and asked for his driver's license for use in a demonstration of a field background check. After he handed them his license, the police ran his information through the system. They learned something interesting. The computer revealed there was an outstanding warrant for the man's arrest for his involvement in a 1986 armed robbery in St. Louis. He was arrested on the spot.

Apparently this crook just couldn't stay away from the cops.

Flame Shame

Three teenage boys tried to use a cigarette lighter to help them steal fuel in the dark. You can guess how well that turned out.

The trio of dimwits—ages 15, 17, and 19—broke into the Mungallala Sawmill in Mungallala, Australia, late one night in 2007 and began taking fuel out of a tank in a shed. During the theft, one of them wondered how much fuel they had already stolen. Because it was dark and they didn't have a flashlight, another one flicked on his cigarette lighter to see.

The flame lit the gas fumes, causing the entire shed to go up in flames, along with the sawmill itself. One of the teens was injured in the blaze, and all three were charged with arson.

Name-dropper

An escapee decided to lie low at a hotel so the cops wouldn't find him. But they did—because he registered under his real name.

The simpleton had been jailed in Tampa, Florida, for violating probation from an earlier grand theft case. As part of a work-release program for inmates, he was allowed to work at a recycling plant in 2006. He was only three and a half months away from being set free when he stupidly walked off the job at 10:45 A.M. and did not return.

Later that day, detectives obtained information that the escapee frequented an area around the Milner Hotel. They went to the hotel and, to their pleasant surprise, found that he had checked in under his actual name. This was just too easy. The cops went to his room and busted him without any problem.

When asked why he escaped, he didn't have an answer. The fool, who would have been free in a few months, now faced the real possibility of having an additional 15 years tacked on to his sentence for felony escape.

About the Author

Allan Zullo is the author of nearly 100 nonfiction books on subjects ranging from sports and the supernatural to history and animals.

He has written the bestselling Haunted Kids series, published by Scholastic, which are filled with chilling stories based on, or inspired by, documented cases from the files of ghost hunters. Allan also has introduced Scholastic readers to the Ten True Tales series, about people who have met the challenges of dangerous, sometimes life-threatening, situations. He is also the author of the original *World's Dumbest Crooks* and *Incredible Dogs and Their Incredible Tales*.

Allan, the grandfather of four and the father of two grown daughters, lives with his wife, Kathryn, on the side of a mountain near Asheville, North Carolina. To learn more about the author, visit his website at www.allanzullo.com.

For more clumsy criminals and
foolish felons, be sure to check out: